"Endowed by Their Creator"

A Collection of Historic American Military Prayers:
1774-Present

Printed in the United States of America
ISBN 978-0-9849409-0-5

Published by
First Principles Press
P.O. Box 1136
Crestwood, KY 40014

We offer this historical case for prayer and the accompanying collection of historic military prayers as hundreds of years of evidence for the necessity of leader-led and chaplain led prayer in America's Armed Forces. May prayer continue to preserve the character of America, providing "liberty and justice for all" and peace and prosperity in our sweet land of the free and home of the brave. In humble gratitude we dedicate this book and honor those whose service and sacrifice has maintained America's Spirit and Liberty since her founding.

Preface

My First American Armed Forces Prayer Book

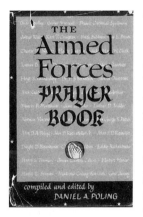

The first American Military Prayer Book I ever saw was given to me by my "Uncle Doc," my father's oldest brother, US Army Captain Manuel Ray. Like his father before him, Manuel, was a mountain doctor, who served in World War II and was the first doctor wounded on Anzio Beachhead in the battle against the Germans, in Italy. Uncle Doc lost his only son, Joseph, in the battle for Okinawa. Little Joe never came home to Hazard, Kentucky, as his body was not recovered. His name is etched, along with all those who lost their lives in the Pacific, during World War II, on the stone of the granite pillars at the Punch Bowl Cemetery in Honolulu, Hawaii.

Before I deployed to Vietnam, Uncle Doc gave me *The American Armed Forces Prayer Book*, 1951. I took this prayer book with me in March 1967, on my way halfway around the world as a Marine Captain, where I served in country as an advisor to the 3rd Vietnamese Marine Infantry Battalion. "Uncle Doc" inscribed a short note inside the front cover of the prayer book – "So you can have your own G.I. Service where there is no church nearby" – I appreciated his gesture and the gift, but I wasn't praying much in those days. Nonetheless, my prayer book gift was kept in a secure place while I was in Vietnam and it accompanied me home.

After 35 years, I found the prayer book again in January 2001. Our son Shelby was on his way to Marine Corps Boot Camp at Parris Island, South Carolina, to prepare for entry into the Virginia Military Institute (VMI), later that year. By that time, I had become acquainted with prayer and knew of God's high purpose for it to glorify Himself as it provided great aid and comfort to man's soul.

Our son graduated from boot camp in the spring of 2001 and entered VMI that August, just prior to 9/11. The following year, in 2002, the ACLU, and others, sued VMI to force the Institute to stop daily mealtime prayers. I found "Uncle Doc's "old prayer book and carefully reviewed it. It contained prayers that were prayed by fighting men of all ranks. The prayer book was recommended for distribution to the Armed Forces during World War II by Presidents, Secretaries of War, Secretaries of State, Admirals, and Generals. More than sixty of the prayers – most of the prayers included – were in the name of Jesus Christ.

From that moment, from that generation to mine, I realized the history of American military prayer was a constant thread. Further research revealed that prayer is vital to the US military, part of our "equipment", as one famous General put it. This belief and confidence in prayer has spanned more than 350 years.

"Uncle Doc's" old prayer book and the understanding it gave to me became the heart of a legal brief I was invited to file in the U.S. Court of Appeals in Richmond, Virginia, on behalf of the Virginia Military Institute. This made the historic case for prayer and its importance as VMI's own General Marshall described it as necessary "equipment" for the soldier. After rival briefs were filed, arguments fell silent and a six to six rehearing *en banc*, opened the way for this case to be appealed to the supreme Court. The Naval Aviation Foundation, First Principles Press, and the Coalition of American Veterans supported the effort to present the unbroken history of prayer in America's Armed Forces to the Court as "Military Necessity" – meaning prayer is as important as ammunition, weapons, chow, water, good order and discipline.

Through our research, I was further impressed to learn that prayer was considered a foundation of the American military particularly by John Adams, who led the military committee that drew up the two first principles of the American military which are 1) Exemplary Conduct; and 2) Daily Prayer:

Article 1. "The Commanders of all ships and vessels belonging to the THIRTEEN UNITED COLONIES, are strictly required to show in themselves a good example of honor and virtue to their officers and men, and to be very vigilant in inspecting the behavior of all such as are under them and to discountenance and suppress all dissolute, immoral and disorderly practices; and also, such as are contrary to the rules of discipline and obedience, and to correct those who are guilty of the same according to the usage of the sea."

Article 2 "The Commanders of the ships of the thirteen United Colonies are to take care that divine service be performed twice a day on board, and a sermon preached on Sundays, unless bad weather or other extraordinary accidents prevent."

The generation that defended the nation in World War II and Korea are now passing in review onto their eternal rest, with so many of their comrades who fell many years ago on battlefields far away in defense of liberty and justice for all. It is now left to us who follow, to hand down American military prayer to the next generation, just as it was given to an ignorant and unsuspecting Marine officer by "Uncle Doc", before leaving for the jungles of Vietnam.

To those who serve today this prayer book is a collection of historic military prayers prayed by the strong, the weak, and seemingly fearless with the intention that you find the long understood joy and wonder of prayer for God's sure protection. He is indeed your refuge, fortress, and trust; He delivers you from the snare as your shield and buckler; He assuages your fear by night and day, so that no evil shall befall you for He has given His angel's charge over you, and while you may not know Him, He knows your name.

Semper Fidelis,
Colonel Ronald D. Ray, USMC (Ret.)
September 11, 2011

Acknowledgments:

The concept for this book took shape and order under the careful and watchful hand of Dr. Linda Jeffrey. She became a relentless collector of historic military prayer books to assist in making the case with Colonel Ronald D. Ray, USMC (ret.) in the Virgina Military Institute (2001-2004).

The historic collection of American military prayers became the heart of a formal Report on the Professional Military Judgment of Senior American Commanders (From 1775 to Present) Concerning the Crucial Importance of Official Prayer to the Morale and Well-Being of the American Military. The Report was accomplished under the direction of Admiral Thomas H. Moorer, USN (ret.), former Chairman of the Joint Chiefs of Staff, Vice Admiral Gerald E. Miller, USN (ret.), Rear Admiral C. A. Hill, USN (ret.) and General Ray Davis, USMC (ret.), on behalf of The Naval Aviation Foundation. This Report became the Appendix to a formal brief filed in support of the Virginia Military Institute in the U.S. Court of Appeals for the Fourth District and the U.S. supreme Court.

Two shepherding individuals, Emily Sears and Krista Gora, added the indispensable requirements of keeping the work on schedule, organizing the gathered research, selecting and editing the content for the historic collection from amongst hundreds of prayers and dozens of prayer books, carefully treading through the layout of the book, culminating with a history of prayer in the U.S. military (1774-present) that comes alive today.

A selection of prayers drawn from those first prayer books filled the first pages of this work. A young Robert "Hardy" Hendren spent the summer, before matriculating at Virginia Military Institute as a rat in the class of 2015, sorting through prayers, collecting more prayer books via used bookstores and internet sites, to add to the growing collection.

His sister, Brigitta Hendren, added to Hardy's efforts by further researching information on the authors of prayers in the collection selected for publication.

We were delighted to have a few talented, young artists, Lindy Ayres, Kellen Ayres and Spencer McCloy, volunteer their time to provide the beautiful, historic drawings found in the Chronology of Wars & Conflicts section. Their depictions of historical events serve as visual reminders of the sacrifices we must never forget.

It is to these dedicated individuals and with the faithful support of friends and donors that we extend our hearty thanks. Without their efforts, we would not have been able to present to you this unique and vitally important collection of historic American military prayers.

– Thank You –

Revelation 7:12
Blessing, and glory, and wisdom, and thanksgiving, and honour, and power, and might, be unto our God for ever and ever. Amen.

Table of Contents

Forward

Cry Restore! (Isaiah 42:22)

In 1942, the U.S. Government Printing Office printed at tax
expense, a copy of the New Testament and Psalms "for the use of
Protestant Personnel of the Army of the United States." These
small pocket-sized Bibles emphasized the prayers of the Psalmist
David, a man well versed in war and the intervening Providence
of Almighty God. President Franklin Roosevelt's comments were
carried on the inside cover, dated March 6, 1941,

> To the Members of the Army: As Commander-in-Chief I take
> pleasure in commending the reading of the Bible to all who
> serve in the armed forces of the United States. Throughout
> the centuries men of many faiths and diverse origins have
> found in the Sacred Book words of wisdom, counsel and
> inspiration. It is a fountain of strength and now, as always, an
> aid in attaining the highest aspirations of the human soul.

In the span of one generation, these precious words from a national
leader have become foreign and alien in the American Armed Forces
where the media reports of disorderly and immoral conduct in the
ranks, which is being promoted and tolerated. Yet, Christian prayers
of military leaders and Christian Chaplains are unable to pray in Jesus'
name or are being completely silenced.

In 2008, First Principles began to collect historic military prayer books
and testimonies which demonstrate the "military necessity" of earnestly
seeking through Christian prayer, the favor of Almighty God over the
United States Armed Forces for more than 230 years.

How important is Prayer on the battlefield? Rod Dreher writing in
National Review, March 10, 2003, says:

> The nearly 1,400 chaplains in the U.S. armed forces – nearly
> all Christian except for about 30 Jewish and 15 Muslim
> clergy – must be on-the-spot counselors to men and women
> living through a kind of trauma that few civilians will ever
> experience…And most important, on the battlefield they serve
> as a sign of the presence of the just and good God in the midst

of hell on earth…To soldiers under fire, the chaplain's presence is a sign that God has not abandoned them…The things soldiers are asked to do and to suffer are so extreme that in many cases, only a belief that God is with them helps them to endure.

A written history of prayer and a collection of military prayers for use by service members and Christian chaplains are needed. With this publication, we have aimed to:

- Present historic evidence of God's Divine Providence in America's military history.
- Provide Chaplains, military leaders and troops with access to an expansive body of prayers included with the rich history of Christian prayer in the American military since the nation's founding.

Seventy-seven prayer books have been published and/or distributed through official U.S. government channels to our fighting forces beginning in 1644 through 2002. Of those seventy-seven Armed Forces Prayer Books, we were able to obtain copies of twenty-eight, in addition to a dozen or so available online.

Out of those prayer books we have collected a select number of historic military prayers on a variety of prayer topics and not surprisingly more than 70% of the prayers in these books either reference or are in the name of Jesus Christ.

We have taken a sample from each of these prayer books and present them here, as a chronology to document the history of prayer in our Armed Forces, to support America's Biblical foundations, and also as a reference tool with prayers identified by subject for use in specific situations and circumstances.

And so, after years of prayer and action, we present a historical collection of American military prayers, drawn from our growing collection of military prayer books distributed to our fighting forces overseas and at home. With these battle-tested, historical prayers, we hope that this book will provide guidance, comfort, and confidence through Jesus Christ for all who serve to protect America as One Nation Under God, whose Official National Motto is, "In God We Trust".

THE NECESSITY OF PRAYER TO EFFECTIVE MILITARY & COMBAT LEADERSHIP

The Necessity of Prayer to Effective Military & Combat Leadership

Introduction

In 2002, The Naval Aviation Foundation (NAF), led by former Chairman of the Joint Chiefs Admiral Thomas Moorer and Admiral Mark Hill, filed a friend of the court brief in the Virginia Military Institute prayer case, *Mellen and Knick v. Bunting*, targeted at removing mealtime prayers at VMI. This would be the first major battle in the war against prayer in the Armed Forces.

VMI was a target because it is state supported and trains young men and women to defend our country "in time of national peril," and thus, it is a part of America's military and defense establishment. The NAF presented many proofs from American history, including organic utterances, official acts, testimonials, and the prayers of America's Commanders-in-Chief and preeminent combat leaders, to reconfirm to the judges that American military leadership considers prayer a "military necessity" and has so from America's founding, to this present hour.

Judges use the term "military necessity," to describe the judicial deference given to America's uniformed military leadership because of the different demands on those charged with winning America's wars and ultimately securing the nation's defense and security.

The country's first organic utterance is the Declaration of Independence. It recognizes the "Creator" and "Divine Providence". The authors of the Declaration also wrote the U.S. Armed Forces' first principles, which form the military's core principles. The "Creator", cited in the Declaration of Independence, is the same "God" called upon in the Armed Forces "sacred oaths," all of which end with the prayer, "…so help me God."

The first principles of the Continental Navy were written by John Adams in 1775 and passed by the Continental congress on November 28, 1775. These same principles were reaffirmed and expanded in 1956 by the U.S. Congress and again for the U.S. Army and Air Force in 1997, and remain to this day unchanged.

The second principle of the Continental Navy states:

> "The Commanders of the ships of the Thirteen United Colonies are to take care that divine service be performed twice a day on board, and a sermon preached on Sundays, unless bad weather or other extraordinary accidents prevent it."

The second principle adopted in the Rules and Regulations of for the Continental Army on Friday, June 30, 1775, states:

> "It is earnestly recommended to all officers and soldiers, diligently to attend Divine Service…"

Prayer and American Military History in battles great and small are inseparable in that prayer has been used to foster a sense of honor, loyalty and devotion to duty in service to God and Country. The recognition of our "Creator" found in the Declaration of Independence, and tens of thousands of official government documents and Americans' national dependence upon His superintending or Divine Providence, is often publicly and officially invoked and acknowledged through public and official prayer by the Commander-in-Chief, elected and appointed officials, and most importantly, America's uniformed and civilian military leadership and authorities. All of whom speak with a single voice confirming that prayer to Almighty God for His provision and protection is a vital national security interest for the United States Armed Forces.

Military prayers have never established, supported, or sponsored a specific religion, but rather have acknowledged Divine Providence in the establishment of the United States of America, and the successes of her Armed Forces.

Virtue & The Soldier's Soul

Virtue is the "animating spirit" of the American military and is the "keynote" of a Commander's sworn duty of exemplary behavior, supervision and correction."[1] Successful armies consist of uniformly disciplined, patriotic, well-trained, obedient soldiers, whose high morale demonstrates a special trust and confidence in the patriotism, valor, fidelity and abilities of their military officers and civilian military leaders.

Distinguished VMI graduate General George C. Marshall, author of "The Marshall Plan" to rebuild Europe after World War II, taught that morale comes from "the religious fervor of the soul." It is the essential element of achieving military objectives, and is ignored at great peril, when soldiers hold only guns and orders, with no strength of virtue. Said Marshall:

> …I look upon the spiritual life of the soldier as even more important than his physical equipment…the soldier's heart, the soldier's spirit, the soldier's soul are everything. Unless the soldier's soul sustains him, he cannot be relied on and will fail himself and his commander and his country in the end.

General George C. Marshall

In 1828, Noah Webster defined "soul" as; "The spiritual, rational and immortal substance in man…which enables him to think and reason, and which renders him a subject of moral government." The soul's training for self-government yields a commensurate level of good order and military discipline. American military services are especially constituted to train effective and disciplined forces, to lead and defend the country "in time of national peril," and must therefore be keen to the soul and the true source of American virtue, honor and patriotism.

---

1 Leland P. Lovette, *Naval Customs Traditions and Usage*, George Banta Publishing Company: Menasha, Wisconsin, 1934, p. 60-61. See U.S. Navy, Naval Justice 18-19 (1945).

When military leaders publicly pray they convey to those under their command their subordination to the institutional moral standard, thereby signaling to the ranks their adherence to the standard's high value of life and their careful consideration to the expenditure of lives and resources in accomplishing military combat objectives.

Leaders can rely upon the military chaplaincy, to an extent, to shoulder the responsibility for the spiritual welfare of the troops, but officers lead by example. Subordination to the Declaration's "Creator" through prayer demonstrates to the ranks that commanders recognize the difficulty in humanly alleviating the morale-depleting stresses attributable to separation from their homes, duty in strange surroundings involving people whose language or customs they do not share, fear of facing dangerous training, deadly combat, new assignments, and other service hardships.

Transmitting the military necessity for public prayer and the precedent for a military moral code familiarizes troops with the military's unique justice system, aids them in determining "lawful" orders, both given and received, and assists in inspiring virtue, honor and patriotism, while suppressing all immorality to, and for, the welfare of those under their command.

In the 1950s, after the Korean War, a Defense Department study of returned POW's reported the extent of their poor performance at Communist hands. Because our "soldiers did not understand the Constitution or the stark differences" between the atheistic Communist system and the rights and freedoms with which Americans are endowed by the "Creator" of the Declaration of Independence, President Dwight Eisenhower issued the U.S. Military "Code of Conduct" to reinforce the individual soldier by reaffirming the American purpose and by adding "under God" to the Pledge of Allegiance. The Code of Conduct memorized by all soldiers included; "never to forget that I am an American fighting man, responsible for my actions, and dedicated to the principles which make my country free. I will trust in my God and in the United States of America."

The recognition of "God" and the "Creator" is in tens of thousands of official American government documents. Divine Providence is often publicly invoked and acknowledged through prayer by our Commanders-in-Chief, who without exception have publicly acknowledged "God" in each of their inaugural addresses. Elected and appointed officials, and most importantly, America's uniformed and civilian military leadership and senior authorities, all speak with a single voice confirming that prayer to "Almighty God" for his provision and protection is vital to national security for all of the United States Armed Forces.

Science Confirms the Military Necessity of Prayer

Not only has prayer been deemed essential in the professional judgment of military leaders, scientific research supports its positive impact on military morale, health and well-being.

The Studies in Social Psychology in World War II Series, produced by the Social Science Research Council, was one of the largest social science research projects in history. Volume II, *The American Soldier, Combat and Its Aftermath*, Princeton University Press, (1949), reported data on the importance of prayer to officers and enlisted infantrymen. Prayer was selected most frequently as the soldier's source of combat motivation. The motivation of prayer was selected over the next highest categories of "thinking that you couldn't let the other men down," and "thinking that you had to finish the job in order to get home again." Not only did enlisted infantrymen mention prayers more often than any other item as helping a lot, but length of combat had no effect on the frequency of responses.

> These data would suggest that combat men who had experienced greater stress were at least as likely to say they were helped by prayer as those who had been subjected to less stress" (p. 176)…[T]he fact that such an overwhelming majority of combat men said that prayer helped them a lot certainly means that they almost universally had recourse to prayer and probably found relief, distraction, or consolation in the process (p. 185).

Military training and "going in harm's way" can result in injury and death. The healing aspects of religion and prayer have also been scientifically noted. Dr. Dale Matthews, a physician with Duke University's Center for the Study of Religion/Spirituality and Health, has published a book on *The Faith Factor: Proof of the Healing Power of Prayer*, and the Duke University Center has produced more than 70 data-based, peer-reviewed papers published in medical and scientific journals. Although the mountain of data is vigorously challenged in humanist journals such as *Free Thought* and *Skeptical Inquirer*, Harold Pincus, former deputy medical director of the American Psychiatric Association, stated that these findings make it clear there are "important connections between spirituality, religion, and health," and medical schools have acted to implement its benefits in physician training.

Prayer at Pivotal Points in American History

The Birth of America & The Revolution

Historically, the military has acknowledged Almighty God as sovereign over the affairs of men, especially men of valor in war time. From General George Washington to the present hour, our Commanders-in-Chief have prayed for God's Providence, and acknowledged His favor upon a military force that is dedicated to defending liberty and justice for all.

The first meeting of Congress in 1774 took place at Carpenter's Hall in Philadelphia and was opened with prayer. There was some argument then as to whether men of such diverse religious views could agree to pray. Mr. Samuel Adams arose and said, "that he was no bigot; and could hear a Prayer from any gentleman of Piety and virtue who was at the same time a friend to his Country." The next morning, September 7, 1774, The Reverend Jacob Duche opened the congressional session with prayer.

John Adams described the prayer to his wife Abigail in a letter, saying he had never heard prayer with "such fervor, such ardor,

2 H. A. Pincus. Commentary: Spirituality, Religion, and Health: Expanding, and Using the Knowledge Base. Mind/Body Medicine, 2 (1997) at 49.

such earnestness and pathos, and in a language so elegant and sublime, for America, for Congress, for the Province of Massachusetts Bay, and especially the town of Boston. It has had an excellent effect upon everybody here."[3]

Thursday, June 28, 1787. Benjamin Franklin delivered a speech to the Constitutional Convention addressing a bitter debate over the representation of individual states in the new government. At the age of 81, he was the senior member of the convention. James Madison recorded his words as follows:

> The small progress we have made after four or five weeks close attendance [sic] and continual reasonings with each other—our different sentiments on almost every question, several of the last producing as many noes as ayes, is methinks a melancholy proof of the imperfection of the Human Understanding....
>
> I therefore beg leave to move—that henceforth prayers imploring the assistance of Heaven, and its blessing on our deliberations, be held in this Assembly every morning before we proceed to business, and that one or more of the clergy of this city be requested to officiate in that service.[4]

The Declaration of Independence, our nation's birth certificate establishes,

> We hold these truths to be self-evident, that all men are created equal, that they are endowed by their Creator with certain unalienable Rights, that among these are Life, Liberty and the pursuit of Happiness.

3 C. F. Adams (Ed.). 1841. Letters of John Adams Addressed to His Wife. Boston: Little & Brown, Vol. I, at 23-24.

4 June 28, 1787. James Madison. Notes of Debates in the Federal Convention of 1787. NY: W. W. Morton & Co. Original, 1787, reprinted, 1987. Vol. I, p. 504. See also, Gaillard Hunt and James B. Scott, Eds. 1920. The Debates in the Federal Convention of 1787 Which Framed the Constitution of the United States of America, Reported by James Madison. New York: Oxford University Press.

The acknowledgment of our Creator stretches across the pages of American history in an unbroken line. The supreme Court affirmed our roots in 1892 by declaring,

> ...no purpose of action against religion can be imputed to any legislation state or national, because this is a religious people. This is historically true. From the discovery of this continent to the present hour, there is a single voice making this affirmation...we find everywhere a clear recognition of the same truth....this is a Christian nation.[5]

George Washington recorded in his Orderly Book on July 9th, 1776,

> The honorable Continental Congress having been pleased to allow a chaplain to each regiment, the colonels or commanding officers of each regiment are directed to procure chaplains accordingly, persons of good characters and exemplary lives, and to see that all inferior officers and soldiers pay them a suitable respect. The blessing and protection of Heaven are at all times necessary, but especially so in times of public distress and danger. The General hopes and trusts, that every officer and man will endeavour to live and act as becomes a Christian soldier, defending the dearest rights and liberties of his country.[6]

General George Washington issued this order from Valley Forge on May 5, 1778,

> If having pleased the Almighty Ruler of the universe to defend the cause of the United American States, and finally to raise up a powerful friend among the princes of the earth, to establish our liberty and independence upon a lasting foundation, it becomes us to set apart a day for gratefully acknowledging the

5 Church of the Holy Trinity v. United States, 143 U.S. 457 (1892).
6 Jared Sparks. *The Writings of George Washington.* Vol. XII. Boston: Ferdinand Andrews, Publisher, 1838, at 401.

divine goodness, and celebrating the important event, which we owe to His divine interposition.[7]

And later that year, Washington wrote,

The hand of Providence has been so conspicuous in all this, that he must be worse than an infidel that lacks faith, and more than wicked, that has not gratitude enough to acknowledge his obligations.[8]

During the Revolution, John Adams wrote to his wife,

Our favorite Dr. Tillotson observes that "in all our concernments we ought to have particular regard to the Supreme Disposer of all things, and earnestly to seek his favor and blessing upon all our undertakings, but more especially in the affairs of war, in which the providence of God is pleased many times in a very peculiar manner to interpose and interest itself, because all war is as it were an appeal to God, and a reference of those causes to the decision of His providence which through pride and injustice and perverse passions of men can receive no other determination."[9]

In 1796, President Thomas Jefferson wrote,

And can the liberties of a nation be thought secure when we have removed their only firm basis, a conviction in the minds of the people that these liberties are the gift of God? That they are not to be violated but with His wrath?[10]

---

7 Henry Whiting. 1844. *Revolutionary Orders of General Washington, Selected from MSS. Of John Whiting*, p. 74. From *America's God and Country* by William J. Federer. Fame Publishing, 1996.

8 The Writings of George Washington, supra., note 2, at 402.

9 Charles Frances Adams. 1898. *Familiar Letters of John Adams and His Wife Abigail Adams, During the Revolution.* Boston: Houghton, Mifflin and Co., at 318.

10 Jefferson, *Notes on the State of Virginia*, 1794, Query XVIII, p. 237

The War of 1812

Andrew Jackson, the victorious Major General in the Battle of New Orleans, wrote of the experience,

> It appears that the unerring hand of Providence shielded my men from the shower of balls, bombs, and rockets, when every ball and bomb from our guns carried with them a mission of death.[11]

On March 4, 1829, Andrew Jackson was inaugurated President of the United States. In his address, he offers a prayer for the nation:

> And a firm reliance on the goodness of that Power whose providence mercifully protected our national infancy, and has since upheld our liberties in various vicissitudes, encourages me to offer up my ardent supplications that He will continue to make our beloved country the object of His divine care and gracious benediction.

The War of 1812 also brought us the words to our National Anthem, penned by Francis Scott Key during the Battle of Baltimore. The concluding verse is a prayer for the nation:

> Oh, thus be it ever, when free men shall stand
> Between their loved homes and war's desolation!
> Blest with victory and peace, may the heaven rescued land
> Praise the Power that hath made and preserved us a nation!
> Then conquer we must, when our cause is just,
> And this be our motto: "In God is our trust."
> And the Star-Spangled Banner in triumph shall wave
> O'er the land of the free and the home of the brave.

---

11 Burke Davis. 1977. *Old Hickory: A Life of Andrew Jackson*. p. 150. NY: Dial Press. Quoting a January 8, 1815 letter to Robert Hays.

Although the Army and the Navy had for some years regarded "The Star-Spangled Banner" as the national anthem, its designation as such first became official by executive order of President Wilson in 1916. This order was confirmed by act of Congress in 1931.

The Civil War

On March 30, 1863, President Abraham Lincoln issued a historic Proclamation Appointing a National Fast Day:

> Whereas, the Senate of the United States devoutly recognizing the Supreme Authority and just Government of Almighty God in all the affairs of men and of nations, has, by a resolution, requested the President to designate and set apart a day for national prayer and humiliation:

> And whereas, it is the duty of nations as well as of men to own their dependence upon the overruling power of God, to confess their sins and transgressions in humble sorrow yet with assured hope that genuine repentance will lead to mercy and pardon, and to recognize the sublime truth, announced in the Holy Scriptures and proven by all history: that those nations only are blessed whose God is the Lord:

> And, insomuch as we know that, by His divine law, nations like individuals are subjected to punishments and chastisement in this world, may we not justly fear that the awful calamity of civil war, which now desolates the land may be but a punishment inflicted upon us for our presumptuous sins to the needful end of our national reformation as a whole people?

> We have been the recipients of the choicest bounties of Heaven. We have been preserved these many years in peace and prosperity. We have grown in numbers, wealth and power as no other nation has ever grown.

> But we have forgotten God. We have forgotten the gracious Hand which preserved us in peace, and multiplied and

enriched and strengthened us; and we have vainly imagined, in the deceitfulness of our hearts, that all these blessings were produced by some superior wisdom and virtue of our own.

Intoxicated with unbroken success, we have become too self-sufficient to feel the necessity of redeeming and preserving grace, too proud to pray to the God that made us!

It behooves us then to humble ourselves before the offended Power, to confess our national sins and to pray for clemency and forgiveness.

Now, therefore, in compliance with the request and fully concurring in the view of the Senate, I do, by this my proclamation, designate and set apart Thursday, the 30th day of April, 1863, as a day of national humiliation, fasting and prayer.

And I do hereby request all the people to abstain on that day from their ordinary secular pursuits, and to unite, at their several places of public worship and their respective homes, in keeping the day holy to the Lord and devoted to the humble discharge of the religious duties proper to that solemn occasion.

All this being done, in sincerity and truth, let us then rest humbly in the hope authorized by the Divine teachings, that the united cry of the nation will be heard on high and answered with blessing no less than the pardon of our national sins and the restoration of our now divided and suffering country to its former happy condition of unity and peace.

In witness whereof, I have hereunto set my hand and caused the seal of the United States to be affixed. By the President: Abraham Lincoln.[12]

---

12 Abraham Lincoln, March 30, 1863, in a Proclamation of a National Day of Humiliation, Fasting and Prayer. James D. Richardson (U.S. Representative from Tennessee), Ed. *A Compilation of the Messages and Papers*

World War I

Having been involved in World War I for less than a year, President Woodrow Wilson set apart October 30, 1917 and May 30, 1918 as days on which the people of the United States were urged to pray for victory:

> Whereas, the Congress and the United States, buy a concurrent resolution adopted on the fourth day of the present month of October, in view of the entrance and our nation into the vast and awful war which now afflicts the greater part of the world, has requested me to set apart by official proclamation a date upon which are people should be called upon to offer concerted prayer to Almighty God for his divine aid in the success of our arms;

> And, Whereas, it behooves the great free people, nurtured as we have been in the eternal principles of justice and of right, a nation which has sought from the earliest days of its existence to be obedient to the divine teachings which have inspired it in the exercise of its liberties, to turn away to the supreme Master and cast themselves in faith at his feet, praying for his aid and succor in every hour of trial, to the end that the great aims to which our fathers dedicated our power as a people may not perish among men, but be always asserted and defended with fresh ardor and devotion and, through the Divine blessing, set at last upon enduring foundations for the benefit of all the free peoples of the earth:

> Now, therefore, I, Woodrow Wilson, president of United States, gladly responding to the wish expressed by the Congress, do appoint October twenty-eighth, being the last Sunday of the present month, as a day of supplication and prayer for all the people of the nation, earnestly exhorting all my countrymen to observe the appointed day, according to their several faiths, in solemn prayer that God's blessing may rest upon the high task which is lay upon us, to the end

---

of the Presidents 1789-1897. 10 Vols. Washington D.C.: U.S. Govt. Printing Office, published by authority of Congress, 1897, 1899.

that the cause for which we give our lives and treasure may triumph and our efforts be blessed with high achievement...[13]

On January 20, 1918, President Wilson, "following the reverent example of his predecessors" enjoined the military and Naval forces to regularly observe the Sabbath:

Such an observance of Sunday is dictated by the best traditions of our people and by the convictions of all who look to Divine Providence for guidance and protection, and, in repeating in this order the language of President Lincoln, the President is confident that he is speaking alike to the hearts and to the consciences of those under his authority.[14]

World War II

World War II has numerous examples of a nation at prayer. Perhaps the most famous instance of prayer in the troops was a circulated prayer by General George Patton in December, 1942. In the interview with Chaplain Brigadier General James H. O'Neill, General Patton confided,

Chaplain, I am a strong believer in prayer...We were lucky in Africa, in Sicily, and in Italy, simply because people prayed. But we have to pray for ourselves, too. A good soldier is not made merely by making him think and work. There is something in every soldier that goes deeper than thinking or working.—it's his 'guts.' It is something that he has built in there: it is a world of truth and power that is higher than himself. Great living is not all output of thought and work. A man has to have intake as well. I don't know what you call it, but I call it Religion, Prayer, or God...We've got to get not

13 President Woodrow Wilson, October 30, 1917, A Proclamation of a National Day of Supplication and Prayer. Bertram Benedict, *A History of the Great War*, Vol. 1. New York: Bureau of National Literature, 1919, p. 386.

14 President Woodrow Wilson, January 20, 1918, A Proclamation for the Military and Naval Forces Observance of Sabbath. Bertram Benedict, *A History of the Great War*, Vol. 1. New York: Bureau of National Literature, 1919, p. 387-388.

only the chaplains but every man in the Third Army to

pray. We must ask God to stop these rains. These rains are the margin that holds defeat or victory...I believe that prayer completes the circuit. It is power.[15]

On December 11th and 12th, 3,200 training letters on prayer were distributed to every chaplain and organizational commander down to and including the regimental level, and 250,000 prayer cards were distributed to every soldier in the Third Army with the now famous Patton prayer:

Almighty and most merciful Father, we humbly beseech Thee, of Thy great goodness, to restrain these immoderate rains with which we have had to contend. Grant us fair weather for Battle. Graciously hearken to us as soldiers who call upon Thee that armed with Thy power, we may advance from victory to victory, and crush the oppression and wickedness of our enemies, and establish Thy justice among men and nations. Amen.

The Chaplain reports, "On December 20, to the consternation of the Germans and the delight of the American forecasters who were equally surprised at the turnabout—the rains and the fogs ceased. For the better part of a week came bright clear skies and perfect flying weather. Our planes came over by tens, hundreds, thousands."[16]

The president throughout World War II, Franklin Delano Roosevelt, took his oath of office on Saturday, March 4, 1933. He prayed in his address,

In this dedication of a Nation we humbly ask the blessing of God. May He protect each and every one of us. May He guide me in the days to come.

---

15 Chaplain James H. O'Neill. 1948. The True Story of the Patton Prayer. *The Military Chaplain*. Vol. 19, No. 2, p. 2.
16 Id., p. 3, 13.

Roosevelt's most famous prayer would come eleven years later, when on D-Day, June 7, 1944, he asked his fellow Americans to join him in prayer for American troops facing the most difficult battle of World War II. As people gathered around their radios for his famous fireside chat, Roosevelt prayed,

My fellow Americans:

Last night when I spoke with you about the fall of Rome I knew at that moment the troops of the United States and our allies were crossing the channel in another and greater operation. It has come to pass with success thus far. And so in this poignant hour I ask you to join with me in prayer.

Almighty God, our sons, pride of our nation, this day have set upon a mighty endeavor. A struggle to preserve our Republic, our religion, and our civilization, and to set free a suffering humanity. Lead them straight and true; give strength to their arms, stoutness to their hearts, steadfastness in their faith.

They will need Thy blessings. Their road will be long and hard, for the enemy is strong. He may hurl back our forces, success may not come with rushing speed. But we shall return again and again. And we know that by Thy grace, and by the righteousness of our cause, our sons will triumph. They will be…. night and day without rest until the victory….

The darkness will be rent by noise and flame. Men's souls will be shaken with the violences of war. For these men are lately drawn from the ways of peace. They fight not for the lust of conquest. They fight to end conquest. They fight to liberate. They fight to let justice arise and tolerance and good will among all thy people. They yearn but for the end of battle, for their return to the haven of home. Some will never return. Embrace these, Father, and receive them Thy heroic servants into Thy Kingdom. And for us at home, fathers, mothers, children, wives, sisters, and brothers of brave men overseas, whose thoughts and prayers are ever with them, Help us almighty God to rededicate ourselves to renewed faith in Thee in this hour of great sacrifice.

Many have urged that I call this nation into a single day of special prayer. But because the road is long, the desire is great, I ask that our people devote themselves in a continuance of prayer. As we rise to each new day, and again when each day is spent, let words of prayer be on our lips invoking thy help to our efforts. Give us strength too. Strengthen our daily tasks. Redouble the contributions we make in the physical and material support of our armed forces.

Let our hearts be stout to wait out the long travail. To bear sorrows that may come. To impart our courage to our sons wheresoever they may be. And, O Lord, give us faith, Give us faith in Thee, faith in our sons, faith in each other, faith in our united crusade.

Let not the keenness of our spirits ever be dull. Let not the impact of temporary events, of temporal matters of but fleeting moments, let not these deter us in our unconquerable purpose. With Thy blessing we shall prevail over the unholy forces of our enemy. Help us to conquer the apostles of greed and racial arrogances. Lead us to the saving of our country and with our sister nations into a world unity that will spell a sure peace, a peace invulnerable to the [unintelligible] of unworthy men, and a peace that will let all men live in freedom, reaping the just rewards of their honest fight. Thy will be done, Almighty God. Amen.[17]

After the Great War's end, an aging Herbert Hoover reflected on "The Meaning of America" on August 10, 1948:

At the time our ancestors were proclaiming that the Creator had endowed all mankind with rights of freedom as the children of God, with a free will, there was being proclaimed by Hegel, and later by Karl Marx, a satanic philosophy of agnosticism and that the rights of man came from the

17 Audio recording transcribed from www.wavethemes.org/!usa/index.html, Franklin Delano Roosevelt, June 7, 1944

State. The greatness of America today comes from the one philosophy, the despair of Europe from the other.[18]

In one of his final addresses to the Republican National Convention on July 8, 1952, approaching his 78th birthday, Mr. Hoover declared, "And I shall continue to fight for those principles which made the United States the greatest gift of God to freedom. I pray to Him to strengthen your hands and give you courage."

General Omar Bradley, the first chairman of the Joint Chiefs of Staff in the newly created Department of Defense, contributed a prayer to the Armed Forces Prayer Book published in 1951. General Bradley wrote:

> "Since my cadet days at the Military Academy I have always gotten a great deal of comfort and consolation from the Cadet Prayer. This prayer is an integral part of cadet life at the United States Military Academy." General James Lawton Collins, Chief of Staff, also named his favorite prayer for inclusion in this book, the Cadet Prayer.

> O God, our Father, Thou Searcher of men's hearts, help us to draw near to Thee in sincerity and truth. May our religion be filled with gladness and may our worship to Thee be natural.

> Strengthen and increase our admiration for honest dealing and clean thinking, and suffer not our hatred of hypocrisy and pretense ever to diminish. Encourage us in our endeavor to live above the common level of life. Make us to choose the harder right instead of the easier wrong, and never to be content with a half truth when the whole can be won. Endow us with courage that is born of loyalty to all that is noble and worthy, that scorns to compromise with vice and injustice and knows no fear when truth and right are in jeopardy. Guard us against flippancy and irreverence in the sacred things of

18 Herbert Hoover. The Meaning of America. August 10, 1948. Homecoming Address at the Reception Tendered by West Branch, Iowa, the President's birthplace.

life. Grant us new ties of friendship and new opportunities of service. Kindle our hearts in fellowship with those of a cheerful countenance, and soften our hearts with sympathy for those who sorrow and suffer. May we find genuine pleasure in clean and wholesome mirth and feel inherent disgust for all coarse-minded humor. Help us in our work and in our play to keep ourselves physically strong, mentally awake, and morally straight that we may the better maintain the honor of the Corps untarnished and unsullied, and acquit ourselves like men in our effort to realize the ideals of West Point in doing our duty to Thee and to our Country. All of which we ask in the name of the Great Friend and Master of men. Amen.[19]

Another World War II General, Dwight David Eisenhower, was elected president in 1953. He began his inaugural address with a prayer for Divine power and discernment:

My friends, before I begin the expression of those thoughts that I deem appropriate to this moment, would you permit me the privilege of uttering a little private prayer of my own. And I ask that you bow your heads:

Almighty God, as we stand here at this moment my future associates in the executive branch of government join me in beseeching that Thou will make full and complete our dedication to the service of the people in this throng, and their fellow citizens everywhere. Give us, we pray, the power to discern clearly right from wrong, and allow all our words and actions to be governed thereby, and by the laws of this land. Especially we pray that our concern shall be for all the people regardless of station, race, or calling. May cooperation be permitted and be the mutual aim of those who, under the concepts of our Constitution, hold to differing political faiths; so that all may work for the good of our beloved country and Thy glory. Amen.

On March 16, 2002, Secretary of Defense Donald H. Rumsfeld, with the "War on Terrorism" underway, reaffirmed the centrality

19 Daniel A. Poling. 1951. *The Armed Forces Prayer Book*. New York: Prentice Hall, at 12-13.

of the unbroken line of the military's first principles, and called for the Armed Forces to renew its attention to the Declaration of Independence and the Constitution,[20] to which every member of the uniformed services takes a sacred oath to "support and defend." Without "God" there is no basis for the "sacred oath" to which Secretary Rumsfeld refers.

Conclusion

That American military spirit borne of the military's first principles, virtue, honor and patriotism, is confirmed in the public prayers, public speeches, and writings of senior military leadership in an unbroken line from the nation's founding to the present. There are prayers found in the speeches and writings of military leaders and published in a plethora of Armed Forces Prayer Books utilized by servicemen through our entire national history, of which only a sampling is hereafter provided. In two of 77 Military Prayer Books identified in preparation for making the case for prayer, thirty-three senior military authorities acknowledged the essential nature of prayer for every member of the armed forces.

President George W. Bush remarked at a National Day of Prayer gathering on May 3, 2001,

> Our country was founded by great and wise people who were fluent in the language of humility, praise and petition. Throughout our history, in danger and division, we have always turned to prayer. And our country has been delivered from many serious evils and wrongs because of that prayer.[21]

The concept that prayer is a private exercise without impact on the common morale is novel and without foundation. The conduct of soldiers is highly regulated with uniformity being a priority for combat readiness. The morale of the unit is dependent upon members deferring their individual interests to the function of the whole. This is not a matter of requiring a certain faith or creed.

---

20 Sol Bloom, *The Story of the Constitution*, House Office Building: Washington, D.C., 1937, p. 79.
21 White House News Release, Office of the Press Secretary, at www.whitehouse.gov.

The consequence of eliminating common prayer has implications for military readiness. General Patton called on all men of faith to pray, and even provided the words for them to voice a request. Chaplain James O'Neill, Chaplain for General Patton and the Third Army wrote, per the request of General Patton, in Training Letter No. 5, "we must urge, instruct, and indoctrinate every fighting man to pray as well as fight . . . This Army needs the assurance and the faith that God is with us. With prayer, we cannot fail."

Historically, the military has acknowledged almighty God as sovereign over the affairs of men, especially men of valor in war. Prayer must not be made into a wedge of exception or treated as a dispensable triviality. Great military leaders as well as our Presidents throughout our history have acknowledged Divine Providence who has created all men equal, and Whose favor has been earnestly sought. Those who cannot participate in this military act, according to General Marshall, are not the soldiers whose souls would sustain them in battle. Prayer is, in law, fact and history, a military necessity, and we offer this collection and case for military prayer now as a form of humble gratitude and honor for the continuous line of shed blood and sacrifice that has maintained the American Spirit and America's Liberty.

CHRONOLOGY OF WARS & CONFLICTS

Chronology of Wars & Conflicts

French and Indian War, 1754-1763

The French and Indian War was fought between Great Britain and France in North America from 1754 to 1763. In 1756, the war erupted into the worldwide conflict known as the Seven Years' War involving Austria, England, France, Great Britain, Prussia, and Sweden. The war was fought primarily along the frontiers between the British colonies from Virginia to Nova Scotia, as the English and the French battled for colonial domination in North America. At the end of the war, France ceded French Louisiana west of the Mississippi River to its ally Spain in compensation for Spain's loss of Florida to Britain, establishing Britain's position as the dominant colonial power in the eastern half of North America.

War for Independence, 1775-1783

The American War of Independence or the American Revolutionary War was fought from 1775-1783. It was a war between the Kingdom of Great Britain and the thirteen British colonies in North America: Delaware, Pennsylvania, New Jersey, Georgia, Connecticut, Massachusetts Bay, Maryland, South Carolina, New Hampshire, Virginia, New York, North Carolina, and Rhode Island.

The Colonies protested the right of the King to tax the Colonies without representation in Parliament. As a result, the Colonies gathered together their own representation, forming the first Continental Congress that would eventually author the Declaration of Independence, proclaiming the United States of America as an independent nation, separate from British rule.

The Treaty of Paris ended the war in 1783. America had achieved independence, with the assistance of France, Spain and the Dutch Republic who desired to inhibit Britain's territorial domination in America. The U.S. at that time covered an area bounded roughly by what is now Canada to the north, Florida to the south, and the Mississippi River to the west.

The War of 1812, 1812-1815

In 1812, James Madison became the first U.S. president to ask Congress to declare war. Once again, the British Empire, one of the world's strongest powers was poised against the United States; however, most of Britain's forces were tied up in the war against Napoleon and France, and very little military assistance could be spared for the defense of Canada. Thus, the two countries were more equally match. In 1814, the British captured and burned Washington, D.C., and later that same year, Francis Scott Key penned the lyrics of our national anthem, "The Star Spangled Banner", after viewing the siege of Ft. McHenry.

The war was fought in three theaters, but the South and the Gulf coast saw major land battles in which the American forces destroyed Britain's Indian allies and Tennessean Andrew Jackson led the defeat of the main British invasion force at New Orleans. The Treaty of Ghent was signed in 1815, bringing an end to the war. While territory was not gained on either side, America had established herself as a self-sustaining force and had repelled the British Empire once again.

Mexican-American War, 1846-1848

The Mexican War began in the wake of the 1845 U.S. annexation of Texas as its 28th state. Mexico considered Texas part of its territory, despite the 1836 Texas Revolution, which resulted in the creation of the Republic of Texas. The major consequence of the Mexican War was the forced Mexican cession of the territories of Alta California –

modern day California, Nevada, Arizona, Utah, western Colorado and southwestern Wyoming – and New Mexico to the U.S. in exchange for $18 million. Mexico accepted the Rio Grande as its new national border.

Civil War, 1861-1865

The American Civil War was the result of decades of tension between the North and South. Following the election of Abraham Lincoln in 1860, tensions escalated and eleven southern states would eventually secede from the United States, forming the Confederate States of America. This left twenty-five states comprising the North, or "the Union". During the first two years of the war, Southern

troops won numerous victories, but their fortunes turned after losses at Gettysburg and Vicksburg in 1863. The Civil War remains the deadliest war in American history with over 600,000 soldiers sacrificing their lives. Iconic heroes came from the Civil War, and they live on in the heart of American today. We remember the faith, bravery, and courage of such men as General Ulysses S. Grant, General Thomas "Stonewall" Jackson, and General Robert E. Lee.

Spanish-American War, 1898

The United States declared war on Spain in 1898 after decades of revolts against Spanish rule in Cuba. The main goal of the conflict was Cuban independence; however, as a result of the war, Spain lost control in the Caribbean, giving up its rights to Puerto Rico, the Philippine Islands, and Guam. The war ended with the signing of the Treaty of Paris in December of 1898.

World War I, 1914-1918

World War I (WWI) was a major war centered in Europe that began in July of 1914, and lasted four years. The world's great powers formed two opposing alliances: the Allies (the United Kingdom, France, Italy, the Russian Empire, and Japan) and the Central Powers (Germany, Austria–Hungary, and Italy). The United States entered the war in 1917 as an "associate power." In all more than 70 million military personnel were mobilized in one of the largest wars in history. More than 9 million soldiers were killed; it was the sixth deadliest conflict in world history. The Allies were victorious. The Treaty of Versailles, signed in 1919, ended the war and determined post-war borders dividing central Europe into several smaller states.

World War II, 1939-1945

Twenty-one years after WWI, a second global conflict arose. Two opposing alliances were formed, similar to WWI, the Axis (Germany, Italy and Japan) and the Allies (France, Poland, the United Kingdom, Canada, Australia, China and the Soviet Union). Germany resolved to conquer and control much of Europe with plans of creating a large German empire in Europe. The

United States did not join the war until 1941, when Japan attacked Pearl Harbor.

The war lasted for six years from 1939-1945 and was the deadliest conflict in world history with an estimated 20 million military lives lost and over 100 million military personnel utilized. Victory was in the hands of the Allies in 1945, with the atomic bomb used to stop Japan and the capture of Berlin by Soviet and Polish troops.

The Cold War, 1946-1991

An "Iron Curtain" fell between Eastern and Western Europe following WWII, dividing the continent into two factions with separate governmental systems and recovering economies. The Soviet Union created the Eastern Bloc enveloping East Germany, Czechoslovakia, Poland, Hungary, Romania, and Bulgaria. The U.S. was instrumental in the recovery of Western Europe and created the North Atlantic Treaty Organization (NATO), with the purpose of binding the military powers of these European countries to repel any future invasion and takeover by communism.

The Cold War was a series of international high tension including two major U.S. Wars: Korea and Vietnam. The Soviet Union collapsed in 1991, bringing an end to the Cold War and leaving the United States as the world's dominant military power.

Korean War, 1950-1953

The Korean War was fought between South Korea, supported by the United Nations, and North Korea, supported by the People's Republic of China (PRC), with aid from the Soviet Union. American administrators divided Korea according to an agreement at the end of World War II along the 38th Parallel, with United States troops occupying the southern part of the country and Soviet troops occupying the northern part. The 38th Parallel became a hostile, political border between the two Koreas. Cross-border skirmishes and raids at the 38th Parallel escalated into open warfare

when North Korean forces invaded South Korea in June of 1950. It was the first significant armed conflict of the Cold War. An armistice brought an end to the war in 1953 after much heavy fighting. Each country involved saw many losses and wounded. China, North Korea, the United Nations and the United States all signed the armistice, yet South Korea refused. The country remains separated to this day.

Vietnam War, 1955-1975

In the 1950's, President Truman approved military assistance for anti-communist efforts in Indochina – Cambodia, Laos and Vietnam. France occupied Indochina, but in 1954 the Viet Mihn defeated the French and elected Ho Chí Minh Prime Minister of North Vietnam, establishing a communist government. In 1955, President Eisenhower deployed military advisors to train and support the South Vietnamese Army. Supported by its communist allies, North Vietnam took up arms against the government of South Vietnam, supported by the United States and other anti-communist nations. U.S. involvement escalated in the early 1960s, with U.S. troop levels tripling in 1961, tripling again in 1962 and the deployment of U.S. combat units in 1965. War would cover all of Indochina. U.S. involvement peaked in 1968 at the time of the Tet Offensive.

Under the Paris Peace Accords, U.S. military involvement ended in 1973; arranged between North Vietnam, the U.S., and reluctantly signed by South Vietnam. Fighting in Vietnam continued for two more years until the capture of Saigon by the North Vietnamese army in 1975. North and South Vietnam were reunified the following year and is today The Socialist Republic of Vietnam. It is estimated that 58,000 American soldiers died in the Vietnam War.

Persian Gulf War/Desert Storm, 1990-1991

The Gulf War was waged by a coalition force of thirty-four nations led by the United States against Iraq in response to Iraq's invasion and annexation of the State of Kuwait. The conflict included an extensive aerial assault on Iraqi troops designed to cripple the military's infrastructure; air power played a defining role in the outcome of the conflict. The aerial assault was followed by a ground assault where the coalition defeated the Iraqi troops in 100 hours. Iraq agreed to the United Nation's permanent cease-fire in April of 1991.

Afghanistan & Iraq, 2001-Present

The "War on Terror" is a military campaign led by the United States and the United Kingdom, with the support of other countries and the North Atlantic Treaty Organization (NATO). The conflicts in Iraq and Afghanistan began in the wake of the September 11 attacks in New York City. On September 20, 2001, President George W. Bush delivered an ultimatum to the Taliban government of Afghanistan and consequently, US forces (with UK and coalition allies) invaded Afghanistan. A few months later, Kabul, the capital city of Afghanistan, fell and the remaining al-Qaeda and Taliban forces retreated to the mountains.

With the fostering of terrorist, militant groups and the belief of the harboring of Weapons of Mass Destruction, the war in Iraq, often referred to as Operation Iraqi Freedom, began in 2003. The U.S. led a ground invasion that quickly led to the fall of Baghdad, the capital city, and the dissolution of Saddam Hussein's regime. Insurgent groups rose up to fight against the U.S. led coalition. Since that time the U.S. and its allies have continued to fight off insurgent attacks, while striving to create a stable economy suitable for self government among the Iraqi people. The U.S. military has remained in Iraq teaching, training and equipping an Iraqi security force.

PRAYERS

1587

O Lord God, when thou givest to thy servants to endeavor any great matter, grant us also to know that it is not the beginning, but the continuing of the same until it be thoroughly finished which yieldeth the true glory; through him that for the finishing of thy work laid down his life. Amen.

Sir Francis Drake
Before the Battle of Cadiz, 1587

Soldiers' and Sailors' Prayer Book, 1944

All Creatures of Our God and King
Francis of Assisi (1225)
Translated: William H. Draper (1926)

All creatures of our God and King
Lift up your voice and with us sing,
Alleluia! Alleluia!
Thou burning sun with golden beam,
Thou silver moon with softer gleam!

Refrain:
O praise Him! O praise Him!
Alleluia! Alleluia! Alleluia!

1644

The Goodness of the Cause

Q. Explain these more particularly and in order, and for it show me what hopes you conceive from the goodness of the cause.

A.   1. A good Cause puts life and courage into men's hearts.

2. A good Cause hath God ever finding with it.

3. A good Cause daunts and dismays the adverse party.

4. A good Cause will undoubtedly prevail at last.

The Souldier's Catechisme: The Parliament's Army, 1644

Before the Throne of God Above
Charitie Lees Smith (1863)

Before the throne of God above
I have a strong and perfect plea.
A great High Priest whose name is Love
Who ever lives and pleads for me.
My name is graven on His hands,
My name is written on His heart.
I know that while in Heaven He stands
No tongue can bid me thence depart.

1774

First Prayer of the Continental Congress

O Lord our Heavenly Father, high and mighty King of kings, and Lord of lords, who dost from thy throne behold all the dwellers on earth and reignest with power supreme and uncontrolled over all the Kingdoms, Empires and Governments; look down in mercy, we beseech Thee, on these our American States, who have fled to Thee from the rod of the oppressor and thrown themselves on Thy gracious protection, desiring to be henceforth dependent only on Thee. To Thee have they appealed for the righteousness of their cause; to Thee do they now look up for that countenance and support, which Thou alone canst give. Take them, therefore, Heavenly Father, under Thy nurturing care; give them wisdom in Council and valor in the field; defeat the malicious designs of our cruel adversaries; convince them of the unrighteousness of their Cause [sic] and if they persist in their sanguinary purposes, of own unerring justice, sounding in their hearts, constrain them to drop the weapons of war from their unnerved hands in the day of battle!

Be Thou present, O God of wisdom, and direct the councils of this honorable assembly; enable them to settle things on the best and surest foundation. That the scene of blood may be speedily closed; that order, harmony and peace may be effectually restored, and truth and justice, religion and piety, prevail and flourish amongst the people. Preserve the health of their bodies and vigor of their minds; shower down on them and the millions they here represent, such temporal blessings as Thou seest expedient for them in this world and crown them with everlasting glory in the world to come. All this we ask in the name and through the merits of Jesus Christ, Thy Son and our Savior. Amen.

Reverend Jacob Duché
Rector of Christ Church of Philadelphia, Pennsylvania
Carpenters Hall, Philadelphia
September 7, 1774

1777

A Chaplain's Prayer

I know you are strong in the might of the Lord. You will go forth to battle on the morrow with light hearts and determined spirits, though the solemn duty may rest heavy on your souls.

And, in the hour of battle, when all around is darkness, lit by the lurid cannon glare and the piercing musket flash—when the wounded strew the ground, the dead litter your path—then remember, soldiers, that God is with you. The eternal God fights for you. He rides on the battle cloud, He sweeps onward with the march of the hurricane charge—God, the Awful and Infinite, fights for you, and you will triumph...

Great Father, we bow before Thee. We invoke thy blessing, we deprecate thy wrath, we return Thee thanks for the past, we ask thy aid for the future. O God of mercy, we pray thy blessing on the American arms. God prosper the cause. Amen.

Joab Prout, 1777
Chaplain of the Continental Army
Before the Battle of Brandywine

Soldiers' and Sailors' Prayer Book 1944

Come Thou Fount of Every Blessing
Robert Robinson (1758)

Come, Thou Fount of every blessing,
Tune my heart to sing Thy grace;
Streams of mercy, never ceasing,
Call for songs of loudest praise.
Teach me some melodious sonnet,
Sung by flaming tongues above.
Praise the mount, I'm fixed upon it,
Mount of Thy redeeming love

1785

A Prayer for a Person Bound to Sea

O Eternal Lord God, who alone spreads out the heavens, and rules the raging of the sea; Be pleased to receive into Thine protection the person of thy servant, for whom our prayers are deferred. Preserve him from the dangers of the sea, (*and from the violence of the enemy;) and may he return in safety to enjoy the blessings of the land, with the fruits of his labours; and with a thankful remembrance of thy mercies, to praise and glorify they holy name, through Jesus Christ, our Lord. *Amen.*

*These words to be said in time of war.

For the Sick

O Lord, look down from heaven, behold, visit, and relieve this thy servant. Look upon him with the eyes of thy mercy; give him comfort, and sure confidence in thee; support him under all trials of his present sickness, relieve his pains, if it seem good unto thee, and keep him in perpetual peace and safety. Through Jesus Christ our Lord. *Amen.*

In the time of War and Tumults

O Almighty God, King of all kings, Governor of all things, whose power no creature is able to resist, to who it belongeth justly to punish sinners, and to be merciful to them that truly repent; Save and deliver us, we humbly beseech thee, from the hand of our enemies; abate their pride, assuage their malice and confound their devices that we, being armed with thy defense, may be preserved evermore from all perils, to glorify thee, who are the only giver of all victory, through the merits of thy only Song Jesus Christ our Lord. *Amen.*

For Peace

O God, who art the author of peace, and lover of concord, in knowledge of whom standeth our eternal life, whose service is perfect freedom; Defend us thy humble servants in all assaults of our enemies, that we surely trusting in thy defense, may not fear the power of any adversaries, through the might of Jesus Christ our Lord. *Amen.*

The Book of Common Prayer 1785, for King's Chapel

Rock of Ages
Augustus Montague Toplady (1776)

Rock of Ages, cleft for me,
Let me hide myself in Thee!
Let the Water and the Blood,
From thy riven Side which flow'd,
Be of Sin the double Cure,
Cleanse me from its Guilt and Pow'r.

Not the labors of my hands
Can fulfill thy Law's demands:
Could my zeal no respite know,
Could my tears forever flow,
All for Sin could not atone:
Thou must save, and Thou alone!

Nothing in my hand I bring;
Simply to thy Cross I cling;
Naked, come to Thee for Dress;
Helpless, look to Thee for grace;
Foul, I to the fountain fly :
Wash me, Saviour, or I die!

Whilst I draw this fleeting breath —
When my eye-strings break in death —
When I soar through tracts unknown —
See Thee on thy Judgment-Throne —
Rock of ages, cleft for me,
Let me hide myself in Thee !

1791

Prayer for Government

We pray Thee O God of might, wisdom, and justice! Through whom authority is rightly administered, laws are enacted, and judgment decreed, assist with Thy Holy Spirit of counsel and fortitude the President of these United States, that his administration may be conducted in righteousness, and be eminently useful to Thy people over whom he presides; by encouraging due respect for virtue and religion; by a faithful execution of the laws in justice and mercy; and by restraining vice and immorality. Let the light of Thy divine wisdom direct the deliberations of Congress, and shine forth in all the proceedings and laws framed for our rule and government, so that they may tend to the preservation of peace, the promotion of national happiness, the increase of industry, sobriety, and useful knowledge; and may perpetuate to us the blessing of equal liberty.

We pray for...all judges, magistrates, and other officers who are appointed to guard our political welfare, that they may be enabled, by Thy powerful protection, to discharge the duties of their respective stations with honesty and ability.

We recommend likewise, to Thy unbounded mercy, all our brethren and fellow citizens throughout the United States, that they may be blessed in the knowledge and sanctified in the observance of Thy most holy law; that they may be preserved in union, and in that peace which the world cannot give; and after enjoying the blessings of this life, be admitted to those which are eternal.

Finally, we pray to Thee, O Lord of mercy, to remember the souls of Thy servants departed who are gone before us with the sign of faith and repose in the sleep of peace; the souls of our parents, relatives, and friends; of those who, when living, were members of this congregation, and particularly of such as are lately deceased; of all benefactors who, by their donations or legacies to this Church, witnessed their zeal for the decency of divine worship and proved their claim to our grateful and charitable remembrance. To these, O Lord, and to all that rest in Christ, grant, we beseech Thee, a place of refreshment, light, and everlasting peace, through the same Jesus Christ, Our Lord and Savior. Amen.

John Carroll, 1791
*First Roman Catholic bishop and archbishop
in the United States. Founder of Georgetown University.*

Amazing Grace
John Newton (1779)

Amazing Grace, how sweet the sound,
That saved a wretch like me....
I once was lost but now am found,
Was blind, but now, I see.

T'was Grace that taught...
my heart to fear.
And Grace, my fears relieved.
How precious did that Grace appear...
the hour I first believed.

Through many dangers, toils and snares...
we have already come.
T'was Grace that brought us safe thus far...
and Grace will lead us home.

The Lord has promised good to me...
His word my hope secures.
He will my shield and portion be...
as long as life endures.

When we've been here ten thousand years...
bright shining as the sun.
We've no less days to sing God's praise...
then when we've first begun.

Amazing Grace, how sweet the sound,
That saved a wretch like me....
I once was lost but now am found,
Was blind, but now, I see.

1814

God of Battles!

O Lord God of Hosts, God of battles! Remember thy servant now. In this need and struggle appear in thy power, and prosper the right and rebuke the wrong. All our help and hope are in Thee. O God of Hosts! God of battles! be gracious unto us, and give courage to these men; give success to our arms; give victory to our country's cause. Amen.

Captain Thomas MacDonough
Before the Battle of Plattsburg, September 11, 1814

Soldiers' and Sailors' Prayer Book 1944

Great is Thy Faithfulness
Thomas Chisolm (1923)

Great is Thy faithfulness, O God my Father;
There is no shadow of turning with thee,
Thou changest not, Thy compassions they fail not,
As thou has been, thou forever will be.

Refrain:
Great is Thy faithfulness!
Great is Thy faithfulness!
Morning by morning new mercies I see
All I have needed Thy hand hath provided
Great is Thy faithfulness, Lord unto me!

Summer and winter and springtime and harvest,
Sun, moon, and stars in their courses above;
Join with all nature in manifold witness,
To thy great faithfulness, mercy, and love.

Pardon for sin and a peace that endureth,
Thine own great presence to cheer and to guide;
Strength for today, and bright hope for tomorrow
Blessings all mine, with ten thousand beside.

1833

Lead, Kindly Light

Lead, Kindly Light, amid the encircling gloom,
Lead Thou me on!
The night is dark, and I am far from home,
Lead Thou me on!
Keep Thou my feet! I do not ask to see
The distant scene; one step enough for me.

I was not ever thus, nor prayed that Thou
Shouldst lead me on;
I loved to choose and see my path; but now
Lead Thou me on!
I love the garish day; and, spite of fears,
Pride ruled my will: remember not past years.

So long Thy power has blest me, sure it still
Will lead me on
O'er the moor and fen, o'er crag and torrent, till
The night is gone;
And with the morn those angel faces smile,
Which I have loved long since, and lost awhile.

Hymn Written in 1833 by John Henry Newman

General Dwight D. Eisenhower,
Commander of West European armies, wrote that his favorite prayer was the Twenty-third Psalm and his favorite hymn "Lead, Kindly Light."
The Armed Forces Prayer Book 1951

Battle Hymn of the Republic
Julia W. Howe (1861)

Mine eyes have seen the glory of the coming of the Lord;
He is trampling out the vintage where the grapes of wrath are stored;
He hath loosed the fateful lightning of His terrible swift sword;
His truth is marching on.
Glory! Glory! Hallelujah! Glory! Glory! Hallelujah!
Glory! Glory! Hallelujah! His truth is marching on.

41

1843

A Prayer for the Navy

O Eternal God, may the vessels of our Navy be guarded by Thy gracious Providence and care. May they not bear the sword in vain, but as the defense to those who do well. Graciously bless the officers and men of our Navy. May love of country be engraven on their hearts and may their adventurous spirits and severe toils be duly appreciated by a grateful nation. May their lives be precious in Thy sight, and if ever our ships of war should be engaged in battle, grant that their struggles may be only under an enforced necessity for the defense of what is right. Bless all nations and kindreds on the face of the earth and hasten the time when the principles of holy religion shall so prevail that none shall wage war any more for the purpose of aggression, and none shall need it as a means of defense. All of which blessings we ask through the merits of Jesus Christ our Lord. Amen.

Philadelphia Navy Yard (1843)
This prayer is offered at the launching of battleships
of the United States Navy. It is an adaptation of a prayer
first offered at the Philadelphia Navy Yard in 1843.

Soldiers' and Sailors' Prayer Book 1944

O For A Thousand Tongues to Sing
Charles Wesley (1739)

O for a thousand tongues to sing my great Redeemer's praise,
the glories of my God and King, the triumphs of his grace!

My gracious Master and my God, assist me to proclaim, to
spread through all the earth abroad the honors of thy name.

1845

A Choice for Good or Evil

Once to every man and nation comes the moment to decide,
In the strife of truth with falsehood; for the good or evil side;
Some great cause, God's new Messiah, offering each the bloom or
blight. And the choice goes by forever 'twixt that darkness and that
light.

By the light of burning martyrs, Jesus' bleeding feet I track,
Toiling up new Calvaries ever with the cross turns not back — New
occasions teach new duties, Time makes ancient good uncouth; They
must upward still and onward, who would keep abreast of truth.

Though the cause of evil prosper, yet 'tis truth alone is strong;
Truth forever on the scaffold, wrong forever on the throne! Yet the
scaffold sways the future, and behind the dim unknown, Standeth
God with the shadow, keeping watch above his own.

James Russell Lowell, 1845
Harvard Law School Alumni, American Poet

The Service Prayer Book, 1940

Jesus Paid it All
Elvina M. Hall (1865)

I hear the Savior say,
"Thy strength indeed is small;
Child of weakness, watch and pray,
Find in Me thine all in all."

Refrain
Jesus paid it all,
All to Him I owe;
Sin had left a crimson stain,
He washed it white as snow.

1861

Prayer for Those Exposed to Danger

ALMIGHTY God, the Saviour of all men, we humbly commend to Thy tender care and sure protection, the set Thy servants who have come forth at the call of their country, to defend its government and to protect its people in their property and homes. Let Thy fatherly hand, we beseech thee, be over us; let Thy Holy Spirit be with us; let Thy good Angels have charge of us; with thy loving kindness defend us as with a shield, and either bring us out of our peril into safety, with a heart to show forth thy praises forever, or else sustain us with that glorious hope, by which alone Thy servants can have victory in suffering and death; through the sole merits of Jesus Christ our Lord. Amen.

For Forgiveness

ALMIGHTY and everlasting God, who hatest nothing that thou hast made, and dost forgive the sins of all those who are penitent; create and make in us new and contrite hearts, that we, worthily lamenting our sins and acknowledging our wretchedness, may obtain of thee, the God of all mercy, perfect remission and forgiveness, through Jesus Christ our Lord. Amen.

Before Battle

O MOST powerful and glorious Lord God, the Lord of hosts, that rulest and commmandest all things; thou sittest in the throne judging right: And therefore we make our address to thy Divine Majesty, in this our necessity, that thou wouldest take the cause into thine own hand, and judge between us and our enemies. Stir up thy strength, O Lord, and come and help us; for thou givest not always the battle to the strong, but canst save by many or by few. O let not our sins now cry against us for vengeance; but hear us thy poor servants begging mercy, and imploring thy help, and that thou wouldest be a defense unto us against the face of the enemy. Make it appear that thou art our Saviour and mighty Deliverer, through Jesus Christ our Lord. Amen.

On Deliverance from Enemies

O ALMIGHTY God, who art a strong tower of defense unto thy servants against the face of their enemies; We yield thee praise and thanksgiving for our deliverance from those great and apparent dangers wherewith we were compassed. We acknowledge it thy goodness that we were not delivered over as a prey unto them; beseeching thee still to continue such thy mercies towards us, that all the world may know that thou art our Saviour and mighty Deliverer; through Jesus Christ our Lord. Amen.

Redeem The Soul of Your Servant

O MOST gracious Father, we fly unto thee for mercy in behalf of this thy servant, here lying under the sudden visitation of thine hand. If it be thy will, preserve his life, that there may be place for repentance: But, if thou hast otherwise appointed, let thy mercy supply to him the want of the usual opportunity for the trimming of his lamp. Stir up in him such sorrow for sin, and such fervent love to thee, as may in a short time do the work of many days: That among the praises which thy Saints and holy Angels shall sing to the honour of thy mercy through eternal ages, it may be to thy unspeakable glory, that thou hast redeemed the soul of this thy servant from eternal death, and made him partaker of the everlasting life, which is through Jesus Christ our Lord. Amen.

For Direction

Direct us, O Lord, in all our doings, with thy most gracious favour, and further us with thy continual help; that in all our works begun, continued, and ended in thee, we may glorify thy holy Name, and finally, by thy mercy, obtain everlasting life; through Jesus Christ our Lord. Amen.

For Unity

O GOD, the Father of our Lord Jesus Christ, our only Saviour, the Prince of peace, give us grace seriously to lay to heart, the great dangers we are in by our unhappy divisions. Take away all hatred and prejudice and whatever else may hinder us from godly union and concord, that as there is but one body and one Spirit, and one hope of our calling, one Lord, one faith, one baptism, one God and Father of us all; so we may henceforth be all of one heart and one soul, united in the holy bond of truth, of faith and charity; and may with one mind and one mouth, glorify thee through Jesus Christ our Lord. Amen.

For Congress

MOST gracious God, we humbly beseech thee, as for the People of these United States in general, so especially for their Senate and Representatives in Congress assembled; that thou wouldest be pleased to direct and prosper all their consultations, to the advancement of thy Glory, the good of thy Church, the safety, honour, and welfare of thy People; that all things may be so ordered and settled by their endeavours, upon the best and surest foundations, that peace and happiness, truth and justice, religion and piety, may be established among us for all generations. These, and all other necessaries for them, for us, and thy whole Church, we humbly beg in the name and mediation of Jesus Christ, our most blessed Lord and Saviour. Amen.

Prayer During Present National Troubles

O ALMIGHTY God, who art a strong tower of defense to those who put their trust in thee, whose power no creature is able to resist, we make our humble cry to thee in this hour of our country's need. Thy property is always to have mercy. Deal not with us according to our sins, neither reward us according to our iniquities; but stretch forth the right hand of thy Majesty, and be our defense for thy name's sake. Have pity upon our brethren who are in arms against the constituted authorities of the land, and show them the error of their way. Shed upon the counsels of our Rulers the spirit of wisdom and moderation and firmness, and unite the hearts of our people as the heart of one man in upholding the supremacy of Law, and the cause of justice and peace. Abate the violence of passion; banish pride and prejudice from every heart, and incline us all to trust in thy righteous Providence, and to be ready for every duty. And oh, that in thy great mercy, thou wouldest hasten the return of unity and concord to our borders, and so order all things that peace and happiness, truth and justice, religion and piety, may be established among us for all generations. These things, and whatever else thou shalt see to be necessary and convenient for us, we humbly beg through the merits and mediation of Jesus Christ our Lord and Saviour. Amen.

Soldier's Prayer Book 1861

For a Sick Person

O Father of mercies and God of all comfort, our only help in time of need; Look down from heaven, we humbly beseech thee, behold, visit, and relieve thy sick servant, for whom our prayers are desired. Look upon him with the eyes of thy mercy; comfort him with a sense of thy goodness; preserve him from the temptations of the enemy; give him patience under his affliction; and, in thy good time, restore him to health, and enable him to lead the residue of his life in thy fear, and to thy glory. Or else give him grace so to take thy visitation, that, after this painful life ended, he may dwell with thee in life everlasting; through Jesus Christ our Lord. Amen.

Soldier's Prayer Book 1861 & Prayer Book for the Camp 1863

The Navy Hymn

Eternal Father! Strong to save,
Whose arm hath bound the restless wave,
Who bidd'st the mighty ocean deep
Its own appointed limits keep:
>> O hear us when we cry to thee
>> For those in peril on the sea.

O Christ! Whose voice the waters heard
And hushed their raging at thy word,
Who walkedst on the foaming deep,
And calm amidst its rage didst sleep;
>> O hear us when we cry to thee
>> For those in peril on the sea!

O Trinity of love and power!
Our brethren shield in danger's hour;
From rock and tempest, fire and foe,
Protect them wheresoe'er they go;
>> Thus evermore shall rise to thee
>> Glad hymns of praise from land and sea…
>> Amen.

Written by Rev. William Whiting in 1860
Composed by Rev. John B. Dykes in 1861
Published in: Soldiers' and Sailors' Prayer Book 1944

A Union Soldier's Prayer

Almighty God! eternal friend!
Before thy sacred throne we bend,
And ask in supplications low,
Thy blessing on our cause bestow.
Thy strength unto our host now send,
And wisdom to our councils lend,
Oh aid our country and its laws,
For thine and freedom's sacred cause.

God of our fathers! hear they cry
Which now ascends to thee on high;
A bleeding nation calls on thee,
To shield the birthright of the free.
Unto thy great decrees we bow,
Thy strength alone can aid us now;
Hear our prayer, O Lord divine,
Be vict'ry ours and glory thine.

Oh! Lord of hosts, supreme in might!
Stretch forth thine arm, defend the right;
Hurl treason from its brazen throne,
Let truth and Justice reign alone.
As Israel pass'd through the sea
In safety, guided Lord by thee,
So lead us through the tide of war,
And thine be praise forevermore.

1862

Thy Name is Love

Jesus we look to thee,
Thy promised presence claim;
Thou in the midst of us shall be,
Assembled in thy name:

Thy name salvation is,
Which here we come to prove;
Thy name is life, and health, and peace,
And everlasting love.

Present we know thou art;
But, O, thyself, reveal!
Now, Lord, let every bounding heart
Thy mighty comfort feel!

O may thy quickening voice
The death of sin remove;
And bid our inmost souls rejoice,
In hope of perfect love!

Hymns for the Camp, 1862

Homeward Bound

Out on an ocean all boundless, we ride,
    We're homeward bound;
Tossed on the waves of a rough, restless tide,
    We're homeward bound;
Far from the save, quiet harbor we've rode,
Seeking our Father's celestial abode,
Promise of which on each he bestowed,
    We're homeward bound.

Wildly the storm sweeps us on as it roars,
    We're homeward bound;
Look! Yonder lie the bright heavenly shores,
We're homeward bound;
Steady, O pilot! Stand firm at the wheel,
Steady! We soon shall outweather the gale,
O how we fly 'neath the loud creaking sail,
    We're homeward bound.
At length, at thy right hand,
May we together stand,
And, with the angel-band,
    Surround thy throne.

The Soldier's Hymn-Book: For Camp Worship, 1862

Fairest Lord Jesus
German, 17th Century

Fairest Lord Jesus, Ruler of all nature,
O Thou of God and man the Son,
Thee will I cherish, Thee will I honor,
Thou, my soul's glory, joy and crown.

Beautiful Savior! Lord of all the nations!
Son of God and Son of Man!
Glory and honor, praise, adoration,
Now and forever more be Thine.

1863

For Forgiveness

O God the Father of heaven, have mercy upon me; keep and defend me.

O God the Son, Redeemer of the world, have mercy upon me; save and deliver me.

O God the Holy Ghost, have mercy upon me; strengthen and comfort me.

Remember not, Lord, mine offences, nor the offences of my forefathers; neither take Thou vengeance of our sins. Spare us, good Lord, spare Thy people, whom Thou hast redeemed with Thy most precious blood, and be not angry with us forever.

From Thy wrath and heavy indignation; from the guilt and burden of my sins; from the dreadful sentence of the last Judgment, good Lord deliver me.

From the sting and terrors of conscience; from impatience, distrust, or despair; from extremity of sickness and pain, which may withdraw my mind from God, good Lord deliver me.

From the bitter pangs of eternal death; from the gates of hell; from the powers of darkness, and from the illusions of Satan, good Lord deliver me.

By Thy manifold and great mercies; by Thy manifold and great merits; by Thine agony and bloody sweat; by Thy bitter cross and passion; by Thy mighty resurrection; by Thy glorious ascension, and most acceptable intercession; and by the graces of the Holy Ghost, good Lord deliver me.

For the glory of Thy name; for Thy loving mercy and truth's sake, good Lord deliver me.

In my last and greatest need, in the hour of death, and in the day of

Judgment, good Lord deliver me.

O Lamb of God, who takest away the sins of the world, grant me Thy peace.

O Lamb of God, who takest away the sins of the world, have mercy upon me.

O God, merciful Father, who despises not the sighing of a contrite heart, nor the desire of such as are sorrowful, mercifully assist my prayers which I make before Thee in all my troubles and adversities, whensoever they oppress me; and graciously hear me, that those evils which the craft and subtlety of the devil or man worketh against me may, by Thy good providence, be brought to naught; that I, Thy servant, being hurt by no persecutions, may evermore give thanks unto Thee in Thy holy Church; through Jesus Christ our Lord. Amen.

For Temperance

Gracious Lord, who hast afforded us the use of Thy good creatures for the refreshment of our bodies, and art the Author and Giver of all good things, give me grace always to use this liberty with thankfulness and moderation, that my table may never be made a snare unto me. And grant that my pursuits may not be after the meat that perisheth, but after that which endureth unto everlasting life; that, hungering and thirsting after righteousness, I may be filled with Thy grace here, and Thy glory hereafter, through Jesus Christ our Lord. Amen.

For Perseverance

O eternal God, who seest my weakness, and knowest the number and strength of the temptations against which I have to struggle, leave me not to myself, but cover Thou my head in the day of battle, and in all Spiritual combats make me more than conqueror through Him that loved me. O let no terrors or flatteries, either of the world or my own flesh, ever draw me from my obedience to Thee; but grant that I may continue steadfast, immovable, always abounding in the work of the Lord; and, by patient continuance in well doing, seek, and at last obtain glory, and honor, and immortality, and eternal life, through Jesus Christ our Lord. Amen.

Look Unto Jesus

He was despised and rejected of men; His life was sought by Herod; He was tempted by Satan; hated by that world He came to save; set at naught by His own people; called a deceiver and a dealer with the devil; was driven from place to place, and had not where to lay His head; betrayed by one disciple, and forsaken by all the rest; falsely accused, spit upon, scourged; set at naught by Herod and his men of war; given up by Pilate to the will of His enemies; had a murderer preferred before Him; was condemned to a most cruel and shameful death; crucified between two thieves; reviled in the midst of His torments; had gall and vinegar given Him to drink; suffered a most bitter death, submitting with patience to the will of His Father.

O Jesus, who now sittest at the right hand of God, to succor all who suffer in a righteous way; be thou my advocate for grace, that in all my sufferings I may follow thy example, and run with patience the race that is set before me. Amen.

For Justice

O Thou King of righteousness, who hast commanded us to keep judgment, and do justice, be pleased by Thy grace to cleanse my heart and hands from all fraud and injustice. Grant that I may most strictly observe that sacred rule of doing unto all men as I would they should do unto me; that I may hurt nobody by word or deed, but be true and just in all my dealings; that so, keeping innocence and taking heed unto the thing that is right, I may have peace at the last, even peace with Thee, through Jesus Christ our Lord. Amen.

For the Fear of God

O most glorious God, who only art high and to be feared, put Thy fear into my heart that I may not sin against Thee, nor sacrilegiously profane any holy thing. O let me never so misplace my fear as to be afraid of man, whose breath is in his nostrils; but fill me, O Lord, with the Spirit of thy holy fear, which is the beginning of wisdom, and keep me in a constant conformity to Thy holy will, that I may, with fear and trembling, work out my own salvation, through Jesus Christ our Lord. Amen.

For Chastity

O holy and immaculate Jesus, who wast conceived in a virgin's womb, and who dost still love to dwell in pure and virgin hearts; give me, I beseech Thee, the grace to keep my heart with all diligence, and to withstand all temptations of the flesh, and with pure and clean heart to follow Thee, the only God, even for Thine own merits' and mercies' sake. Amen.

For the Love of God

O God, who hast prepared for those who love Thee such good things as pass man's understanding, pour into our hearts such love toward Thee that we, loving Thee above all things, may obtain Thy promises, which exceed all that we can desire; through Jesus Christ our Lord. Amen.

For Charity

O Lord, who hast taught us that all our doings without charity are worth nothing, send Thy Holy Ghost, and pour into our hearts that most excellent gift of charity, the very bond of peace and of all virtues, without which whosoever liveth is counted dead before Thee, Grant this for Thine only Son Jesus Christ's sake. Amen.

For the Members of Our Family from Whom We are Separated

O God, merciful and gracious, who art everywhere present, let thy loving mercy and compassion descend upon the heads of Thy servants, the members of my family from whom I am now separated; depute Thy holy angels to guard their persons, Thy holy spirit to guide their souls, Thy providence to minister to their necessities; let Thy blessing be upon them night and day; sanctify them in their bodies, souls and spirits; keep them unblamable to the coming of the Lord Jesus, and make them and me to dwell with Thee forever in the light of Thy countenance, and in Thy glory for Jesus' sake. Amen.

For Thankfulness

Most gracious and bountiful Lord, who fillest all things living with good, and hast taught us that it is a joyful and pleasant thing to be thankful, suffer me not, I beseech Thee, to lose my part in that divine pleasure, but grant that as I daily receive blessings from Thee, so may I daily, from an affectionate and devout heart, offer up thanks to Thee; let Thy mercies lead me to repentance, and give me grace to improve them all to the advancement of Thy glory, and the furtherance of my salvation, through Jesus Christ our Lord. Amen.

Thankfulness, Patience & Courage

O Lord, I give Thee humble and hearty thanks for Thy great mercy in bringing me back from the grave. What Thou hast further for me to do or to suffer, Thou alone knowest: Lord, give me patience and courage, and all Christian resolution and grace to do Thee service. And now that Thou hast mercifully restored me, let me live to love, to honor, and to obey Thee, and all this through Jesus Christ. Amen.

A Form of Thanksgiving After Victory

If the Lord had not been on our side, now may we say; if the Lord himself had not been on our side when men rose up against us;

They had swallowed us up quick, when they were so wrathfully displeased at us.

Yea, the waters had drowned us, and the stream had gone over our souls: the deep waters of the proud had gone over our souls.

But praised be the Lord, who hath not given us over as a prey unto them.

The Lord hath wrought a mighty salvation for us.

We got not this by our own sword, neither was it our own arm that saved us; but Thy right hand, and Thine arm, and the light of Thy countenance, because Thou hadst a favor unto us.

The Lord hath appeared for us; the Lord hath covered our heads, and made us to stand in the day of battle.

The Lord hath appeared for us; the Lord hath overthrown our enemies, and dashed in pieces those that rose up against us.

Therefore, not unto us, O Lord, not unto us; but unto Thy name be given the glory.

The Lord hath done great things for us; the Lord hath done great things for us whereof we rejoice.

Our help standeth in the name of the Lord, who hath made heaven and earth.

Blessed be the name of the Lord from this time forth for evermore.

Glory be to the Father, and to the Son, and to the Holy Ghost.

As it was in the beginning, is now, and ever shall be, world without end. Amen.

Christ Our Refuge

Jesus, Saviour of my soul,
Let me to Thy bosom fly,
While the waves of trouble roll,
While the tempest still is high:
Hide me, O my Saviour, hide,
Till the storm of life is past;
Safe into the haven guide;
O receive my soul at last.

Other refuge have I none,
Hangs my helpless soul on Thee,
Leave, ah, leave me not alone;
Still support and comfort me:
All my trust on Thee is stayed,
All my hope from Thee I bring;
Cover my defenseless head
With the shadow of Thy wing.

For Faith

O blessed Lord, whom without faith it is impossible to please, let Thy
Spirit, I beseech Thee, work in me such a faith as may be acceptable
in Thy sight, even such as may show itself by my works, that it may
enable me to overcome the world, and conform me to the image of
that Christ on whom I believe; that so at the last I may receive the end
of my faith, even the salvation of my soul, by the same Jesus Christ
our Lord. Amen.

For Contentedness

O God, Heavenly Father, who by Thy Son Jesus Christ hast promised to all them that seek Thy kingdom and its righteousness all things necessary to their bodily sustenance, let me always fully resign myself to Thy disposal, having no desires of my own, and teach me in whatsoever state I am therewith to be content. Grant me grace to forsake all covetous desires, and inordinate love of riches, and so to pass through things temporal that I finally lost not the things eternal; through Jesus Christ our Lord. Amen.

The Confederate Soldier's Pocket Manual of Devotions 1863

For Persons Under Affliction

O MERCIFUL God, and heavenly Father, who hast taught us in Thy Holy Word that Thou dost not willingly afflict or grieve the children of men; Look with pity, we beseech Thee, upon the sorrows of Thy servants, for whom our prayers are desired. In Thy wisdom, Thou hast seen fit to visit them with trouble, and to bring distress upon them. Remember them, O Lord, in Mercy; sanctify thy fatherly correction to them; endue their souls with patience under their affliction, and with resignation to thy blessed will, comfort them with a sense of Thy goodness; lift up Thy countenance upon them, and give them peace; through Jesus Christ our Lord. Amen.

A Prayer of Cleansing

ALMIGHTY God, unto whom all hearts are open, all desires known, and from whom no secrets are hid: Cleanse the thoughts of our hearts by the inspiration of thy Holy Spirit, that we may perfectly love thee, and worthily magnify thy holy Name; through Christ our Lord. Amen.

A Prayer for All Conditions of Men

O GOD, the Creator and Preserver of all mankind, we humbly beseech thee for all sorts and conditions of men; that thou wouldst be pleased to make thy ways known unto them, thy saving health unto all nations. More especially we pray for the holy Church universal; that it may be so guided and governed by thy good Spirit, that all who profess and call themselves Christians may be led into the way of truth, and hold the faith in unity of spirit, in the bond of peace, and in righteousness of life. Finally, we commend to thy fatherly goodness all those who are in any way afflicted, or distressed, in mind, body, or estate; that may please thee to comfort and relieve them according to their several necessities; giving them patience under their sufferings, and a happy issue out of all their afflictions. And this we beg for Jesus Christ's sake. Amen.

Prayer Book for the Camp 1863

A General Thanksgiving

Almighty God, Father of all mercies, we, Thine unworthy servants, do give thee most humble and hearty thanks for all thy goodness and loving-kindness to us, and to all men. We bless thee for our creation, preservation, and all the blessings of this life; but above all, for Thine inestimable love in the redemption of the world by our Lord Jesus Christ; for the means of grace, and for the hope of glory. And we beseech thee, give us that due sense of all thy mercies, that our hearts may be unfeignedly thankful, and that we may show forth thy praise, not only with our lips, but in our lives; by giving up ourselves to thy service, and by walking before thee in holiness and righteousness all our days; through Jesus Christ our Lord, to whom, with thee and the Holy Ghost, be all honour and glory, world without end. Amen.

Prayer Book for the Camp 1863,
Armed Forces Hymnal 195X,
& A Prayer Book For the Armed Forces 1988

1864

The Unseen Battlefield

There is an unseen battle-field
In every human breast,
Where two opposing forces meet,
And where they seldom rest.

That field is veiled from mortal sight;
'Tis only seen by One
Who knows alone where victory lies,
When each day's fight is done.

One army clusters strong and fierce,
Their chief of demon form:
His brow is like the thunder-cloud,
His voice, the bursting storm.

His Captains — Pride, and Lust, and Hate —
Whose troops watch night and day,
Swift to detect the weakest point,
And thirsting for the prey.

Contending with this mighty force,
Is but a little band;
Yet there, with an unquailing front,
Those warriors firmly stand!

Their leader is God-like form,
Of countenance serene;
And glowing on His loving breast,
A naked cross is seen.

His Captains — Faith, and Hope, and Love —
Point to that wondrous sign;
And gazing on it, all receive
Strength from a source Divine.

They feel it speaks a glorious truth,
A truth as great as sure —
That to be victors they must learn to love, confide, endure.

That faith sublime, in wildest strife,
Imparts a holy calm;
For every deadly blow a shield,
For every wound a balm.

And when they win the battlefield,
Past toil is quite forgot;
That plain where carnage once had reigned,
Becomes a hallowed spot:

A spot where flowers of joy and peace
Spring from the fertile sod,
And breathe the perfume of their praise
On every breeze — to God.
--Anon.

A Prayer of Comfort

O Father of mercies, and the God of all comfort, our only help
in time of need; we fly unto Thee for succor in behalf of this Thy
servant, here lying under Thy hand in great weakness of body.
Look graciously upon him, O Lord; and the more the outward man
decayeth, strengthen him, we beseech Thee, so much the more
continually with Thy grace and Holy Spirit in the inner man. Give
him unfeigned repentance for all the errors of his life past, and
steadfast faith in Thy Son Jesus; that his sins may be done away
by Thy mercy, and his pardon sealed in heaven before he go hence
and be no more seen. We know, O Lord, that there is no word
impossible with Thee; and that, if Thou wilt, Thou canst even yet
raise him up, and grant him a longer continuance amongst us; yet
forasmuch as in all appearance the time of his dissolution draweth
near, so fit and prepare him, we beseech Thee, against the hour of
death, that after his departure hence in peace, and in Thy favor, his
soul may be received into Thine everlasting kingdom; through the
merits and meditations of Jesus Christ, Thine only Son, our Lord
and Saviour. Amen.

O Lord, I give Thee humble and hearty thanks for Thy great mercy
in bringing me back from the grave. What Thou hast further for me
to do or to suffer, Thou alone knowest: Lord, give me patience and
courage, and all Christian resolution and grace to do Thee service.
And now that Thou hast mercifully restored me, let me live to
love, to honor, and to obey Thee, and all this through Jesus Christ.
Amen.

The Manner of Commending the Sick into the Hands of God at the Hour of Death.

God the Father, who hath created thee, God the Son, who hath redeemed thee, God the Holy Ghost, who hath infused His grace into thee, be now and evermore thy defense, assist thee in this thy last trial, and bring thee into the way of everlasting life. Amen.

Into Thy merciful hands, O heavenly Father, we commend the soul of Thy servant now departing; acknowledge, we beseech Thee, a sheep of Thine own fold, a lamb of Thine own flock. Receive him into the arms of Thy mercy, into the sacred rest of everlasting peace, and into the glorious estate of Thy chosen saints in heaven. O Father Almighty, receive and forgive. O Holy Ghost the Comforter, comfort him in the dark valley of the shadow of death. O Saviour of the world, who by Thy cross and precious blood hast redeemed him, save and help this Thy departing servant, O Lord. Amen.

Balm for the Weary and the Wounded 1864

Crown Him with Many Crowns
Matthew Bridges (1851)

Crown Him with many crowns, the Lamb upon His throne.
Hark! How the heavenly anthem drowns all music but its own.
Awake, my soul, and sing of Him who died for thee,
And hail Him as thy matchless King through all eternity.

1917

For the Air Force

O God, Creator and Upholder of all things; Who by Thy wisdom and power hast enabled men by invention and skill to adventure the regions above the earth: We beseech Thee, Who art present everywhere, keep in Thy sustaining care all who are in our Air Force, or whose duty or employment is in this service, that they may have the safety of Thy protection and now and always praise Thee for Thy fatherly love; through Jesus Christ, our Lord. Amen.

Abundance of Thy Mercy

Almighty and Everlasting God, Who art always more ready to hear than we to pray, and wont to give more than either we desire or deserve: Pour down upon us the abundance of Thy mercy, forgiving us those things whereof our conscience is afraid, and giving us those good things which we are not worthy to ask, but through the merits and mediation of Jesus Christ, Thy son, our Lord. Amen.

For the Success of our Arms

O Lord God of our salvation, we beseech Thee to go forth with our Army and Navy and Air Force, and, by Thy right hand and Thy mighty arm, gain for them the victory, that righteousness may be victorious, the peace which is pleasing to Thee may everywhere prevail, the reign of violence be destroyed and the way be made ready for the coming of that kingdom, before which all earthly might must fall; through Jesus Christ, Thy Son, our Lord. Amen.

For Soldiers and Sailors

Almighty God, Who art the Shield of the righteous: Bless, we beseech Thee, the men who are enlisted in the service of the Nation; grant them courage and devotion to fulfill their duty, the spirit of obedience to their superiors and protection in the hour of danger; through Jesus Christ, Thy Son, our Lord. Amen.

For the Army

O God, Who art a Shield and Buckler to all those that trust in Thee: Stretch forth Thy mighty hand over us Thy servants and the Army in which we serve; lead us and guide us by Thy good Spirit, strengthen and defend us by Thy might, that we may by to our Land a sure defense against every enemy and may enter finally into Thine eternal kingdom; through Jesus Christ, Thy Son, our Lord. Amen.

Before Battle

Heavenly Father, I know Thou art very near me, and in this hour I beseech Thee to receive my humble confession of all the sin and wrong which I have done, and graciously to forgive me for Jesus' sake; give me courage and strength for this hour to go forward trusting wholly in Thee, that whether I live or die, I am Thine, with Thee, in Thy care, now and eternally. Amen.

After Battle

Our Father, Who art in Heaven, Thou hast been my Help and Protection; I humbly give Thee my worship and thanks that Thou hast been with me and preserved me through these hours of danger and brought me forth again in safety; let me never be unmindful of these Thy mercies and help me to show forth, by a life devoted to Thy service, the fullness of my thankful heart; through Jesus Christ, Thy Son, our Lord. Amen.

For the Church

O Lord, favorably receive the prayers of Thy church, that being delivered from all adversity and error, it may serve Thee in safety and freedom: and grant us Thy peace in our time; through Jesus Christ, Thy Son, our Lord. Amen.

For Courage

Teach me, O Master, the courage with which Thou didst face Thy every duty and trial, the consecration with which Thou didst make Thy every sacrifice, that heartened by Thy blessed example, I may never waver in duty, danger or sacrifice, but as a good soldier of the Cross be enabled the better to serve the Country that I love; Who livest and reignest, etc.

In Temptation and Danger

O God, Who seest that of ourselves we have no strength: Keep us both outwardly and inwardly; that we may be defended from all adversities which may happen to the body, and from all evil thoughts which may assault and hurt the soul; through Jesus Christ, Thy Son, our Lord. Amen.

For a Peaceful Death

Confirm, I beseech Thee, Almighty God, Thine unworthy servant in Thy grace; that in the hour of my death the adversary may not prevail against me, but that I may be found worthy of everlasting life; through Jesus Christ, Thy Son, our Lord. Amen.

Redemption of Our Enemies' Soul

O Almighty, Everlasting God, Who, through Thine Only Son, our blessed Lord, hast commanded us to love our enemies, to do good to them that hate us, and to pray for them that persecute us: We earnestly beseech Thee that by Thy gracious visitation they may be led to true repentance and may have the same love, and be one accord, and of one mind and heart with us, and with Thy whole Church; through the same Jesus Christ, Thy Son, our Lord. Amen

Against the Enemies of the Nation

O Lord God Almighty, Who alone riddest away tyrants and stillest the noise and tumult of the people: Scatter, we beseech thee, the counsels of them that secretly devise mischief, and bring the dealings of the violent to naught; cast down the unjust from high places and cause the unruly to cease from troubling; put down all envious and malicious passions and subdue the haters and evil-doers, that the whole world may have rest before Thee and that all nations may serve Thee; through Jesus Christ, Thy Son, our Lord. Amen.

For Those Living in Sin

O Lord Jesus Christ, Who didst come to seek and save the lost: Have pity, we implore Thee, on all miserable captives held in the bondage of vice, lust and intemperance, delivering them from the tyranny of that blind and wicked spirit which defileth their lives and driveth them into all manner of shameful deeps; move their hearts by Thy Spirit, strengthening them to resist and overcome their besetting sin, and lead them into the liberty and purity of the sons of God; Who livest and reignest with the Father and the Holy Ghost, ever One God, world without end. Amen

For Those Who Have Forsaken the Faith

Almighty and Merciful God and Father, we humbly beseech Thee
to visit all those who have forsaken the Christian Faith and to reveal
unto them their error, so that they may receive the Truth of Thy Holy
Word, and walk in the Way that leadeth unto eternal life; through the
same Jesus Christ, Thy Son, our Lord. Amen.

Army and Navy Service Book 1917

For Protection

Almighty God, who seest that we have no power of ourselves to help
ourselves; Keep us both outwardly in our bodies and inwardly in
our souls that we may be defended from all adversities which may
happen to the body, and from all evil thoughts which may assault
and hurt the soul; through Jesus Christ our Lord. *Amen.*

O God, who knowest us to be set in the midst of so many and
great dangers, that by reason of the frailty of our nature we cannot
always stand upright; Grant to us such strength and protection as
may support us in all dangers, and carry us through all temptations;
through Jesus Christ our Lord. *Amen.*

O Almighty Lord and everlasting God, vouchsafe, we beseech Thee,
to direct, sanctify, and govern, both our hearts and bodies in the
ways of Thy laws, and in the works of Thy commandments; that
through Thy most mighty protection, both here and ever, we may
be preserved in body and soul; through our Lord and Saviour Jesus
Christ. *Amen.*

Into Thy hands we commit ourselves, O God. We say of the Lord:
Thou art our refuge, our present help in time of trouble; our hiding-
place from the wind and covert from the temptest; our God, in thee
will we trust; through Jesus Christ our Lord. *Amen.*

For Soldiers and Sailors:
An Abridgment of the Book of Common Worship 1917

For Forgiveness

Grant, we beseech Thee, merciful Lord, to Thy faithful people pardon and peace, that they may be cleansed from all their sins, and serve Thee with a quiet mind; through Jesus Christ, Thy Son, our Lord. Amen.

For Divine Guidance

Direct us, O Lord, in all our doings, with Thy most gracious favor, and further us with Thy continual help; that in all our works begun, continued, and ended in Thee, we may glorify Thy holy Name; and finally, by Thy mercy, obtain everlasting life through Jesus Christ, Thy Son, our Lord. Amen.

For Grace to Love and Serve God

O Almighty God, Whom to know is everlasting life: Grant us perfectly to know Thy Son Jesus Christ to be the Way, the Truth, and the Life; that following His steps we may steadfastly walk in the way that leadeth to eternal life; through the same Jesus Christ, Thy Son, our Lord. Amen.

For Holiness

O God, the Protector of all that trust in Thee, without whom nothing is strong, nothing is holy: Increase and multiply upon us Thy mercy; that Thou being our Ruler and Guide, we may so pass through things temporal, that we finally lose not the things eternal; through Jesus Christ, Thy Son, our Lord. Amen.

For Purity

Almighty God, unto Whom all hearts are open, all desires known, and from Whom no secrets are hid: Cleanse the thoughts of our hearts by the inspiration of Thy Holy Spirit, that we may perfectly love Thee, and worthily magnify Thy Holy Name; through Jesus Christ, Thy Son, our Lord. Amen.

For the Holy Spirit

Send, we beseech Thee, Almighty God, Thy holy Spirit into our hearts, that He may rule and direct us according to Thy will, comfort us in all our temptations and afflictions, defend us from all error, and lead us into all truth; that we, being steadfast in the faith, may increase in love and in all good works, and in the end obtain everlasting life through Jesus Christ, Thy Son, our Lord. Amen.

For the President (or the King), and Those in Authority

Everlasting God, Almighty King, we humbly implore Thee to regard the head of our Government, (N.).......[sic], the President of the United States, or our gracious King George, his counselors, and all others in authority over us, that they, guided by Thy Holy Spirit, may be sure in counsel, unwavering in duty, high in purpose, and so administer their solemn charge as will wholly serve Thy will, uphold the honor of our Nation, make for the care and secure the protection of our people, and bring victory to our righteous cause; through Jesus Christ, Thy Son, our Lord. Amen.

For the Officers of the Army and Navy

Almighty God, Who art the King of kings and the Lord of all power: Bless, we beseech Thee, the Officers of the Army and Navy and Air Force; grant that, submitting their wills to Thy direction, they may be the executives of justice and the ministers of righteousness; through Jesus Christ, Thy Son, our Lord. Amen.

For Our Loved Ones

O Lord God, we humbly beseech Thee to bless and keep our kindred and friends, from whom we are separated in this time of war; and grant that having been again united, we may be one in Thy praise, giving Thee thanks for all Thy mercies and tender care; through Jesus Christ, Thy Son, our Lord. Amen.

For the Navy

O Lord Jesus Christ, at Whose word of peace the waves of the sea were still; Preserve us Thy servants and the Navy in which we serve, from the perils of the great waters and the snares and violence of the enemy, that we may guard our Land against all those that would destroy or straiten its liberties so that all the inhabitants thereof may have peace and freedom to serve Thee; through Jesus Christ, Thy Son, our Lord. Amen.

For Advent

Stir Up, O Lord, we beseech Thee, Thy power, and come, grace whatsoever is hindered by our sins may be speedily accomplished, through thy mercy and satisfaction; Who livest and reignest with the Father and the Holy Ghost, ever One God, world without end. Amen.

For Christmas

O God, Who didst make the holy night of Christ's Nativity shine
with the brightness of the true Light: Grant, we beseech Thee, that
as we have known on earth the mysteries of that Light, we may also
come to the fullness of His joys in heaven; through the same Jesus
Christ, Thy Son, our Lord. Amen.

For Epiphany

O God, Who by the leading of a star, didst manifest Thy Only-
begotten Son to the Gentiles: Mercifully grant, that we, who know
Thee now by faith, may after this life have the fruition of Thy
glorious Godhead; through the same Jesus Christ, Thy Son, our
Lord. Amen.

For Lent

Almighty and Everlasting God, Who hast sent Thy Son, our Saviour
Jesus Christ, to take upon Him our Flesh, and to suffer death upon
the Cross, that all mankind should follow the example of His great
humanity: Mercifully grant that we may both follow the example
of His patience, and also be made partakers of His resurrection;
through the same Jesus Christ, Thy Son, our Lord. Amen.

For Good Friday

Merciful and Everlasting God, Who hast not spared Thine only
Son, but delivered Him up for us all, that He might bear our sins
upon the Cross: Grant that our hearts may be so fixed with steadfast
faith in Him that we may not fear the power of any adversaries;
through the same Jesus Christ, Thy Son, our Lord. Amen.

For Easter

Almighty God, Who, through Thine Only-begotten Son, Jesus Christ, hast overcome death, and opened unto us the gate of everlasting life: We humbly beseech Thee, that as Thou dost put into our minds good desires, so by Thy continual help we may bring the same to good effect; through the same Jesus Christ, Thy Son, our Lord. Amen.

For Ascensiontide

Grant, we beseech Thee, Almighty God, that like as we do believe Thy Only-begotten Son, our Lord Jesus Christ, to have ascended into the heavens; so may we also in heart and mind thither ascend, and with Him continually dwell; Who liveth and reigneth with Thee and the Holy Ghost, ever One God, world without end. Amen.

For Pentecost

O God, Who didst teach the hearts of Thy faithful people, by sending to them the light of Thy Holy Spirit: Grant us by the same Spirit to have a right judgment in all things, Christ Thy Son, our Lord. Amen.

God, Be Near

O Lord Jesus Christ, Who by Thy purity and patience under suffering didst hallow earthly pain and give us an example of holy obedience to the Father's will: Be near me, I pray Thee, in the hours of weakness and pain: sustain me by Thy grace that my strength and courage fail not; grant me patience and heal me, if it be Thy will; and help me ever to believe that what may befall my body is but of little moment if Thou but hold my soul in life, O my Lord and Saviour, Who livest and reignest, etc.

A Prayer for Restoration of Health

Almighty, Everlasting God, the eternal Salvation of them that believe: Hear our prayers in behalf of Thy servants who are sick, wounded and in sore distress, for whom we implore the air of Thy mercy, that being restored to health, they may render thanks to Thee in Thy Church; through Jesus Christ, Thy Son, our Lord. Amen.

For Those Who Minister to the Sick and Wounded

O Most Merciful Father, Who dost commit to our love and care of fellow-men in their necessities: Graciously be with and prosper all those who, after the example of the Good Samaritan, are seeking and ministering to the sick and wounded, let their ministry be abundantly blessed in bringing ease to the suffering, comfort to the sorrowing and peace to the dying, and themselves be inspired with the consecration to selfless service, knowing that inasmuch as they do it unto the least of the Master's brethren, they do it unto Him, Who liveth and reigneth with Thee and the Holy Ghost, ever One God, world without end. Amen.

In Loneliness

Blessed Lord Jesus, Who knowest the depths of loneliness and the dark hours of the absence of human sympathy and friendliness: Help me to pass the weary hours of the night and the heavy hours of the day, as Thou didst, and know that Thou art with me, as Thy Father was with Thee; lift up my heart to full communion with Thee; strengthen me for my duty, keep me constant to my trust, and let me know that however dark or desolate the hour, I am not alone, for Thou art with me; Thy rod and Thy staff be my comfort; Who livest and reignest, etc.

In Affliction

Almighty and most Merciful God, who hast appointed us to endure
sufferings and death with our Lord Jesus Christ, before we enter
with Him into eternal glory: Grant me grace at all times to subject
myself to Thy holy will, and to continue steadfast in the true faith
unto the end of my life, and at all times to find peace and joy in the
blessed hope of the resurrection of the dead, and of the glory of the
world to come; through the same Jesus Christ, Thy Son, our Lord.
Amen.

For Protection During the Night

Lighten our darkness, we beseech Thee, O Lord; and by Thy great
mercy defend us from all perils and dangers of this night; for the
love of Thy Only Son, our Saviour, Jesus Christ. Amen.

For Victory

O God, Whose ears are open unto the prayers of the righteous, but
Whose face is against them that do evil: Help us by Thy Holy Spirit
so to live and to act in accordance with Thy will that we may receive
Thy blessing, and that as, by Thine aid, we overcome our own sins,
we may also by Thy help obtain the victory; through Jesus Christ,
Thy Son, our Lord. Amen.

For Time of War

Father of mercies and God of all comfort, Who in all our affliction
are afflicted; look in pity upon all who are suffering in this time of
strife and warfare of nations. Protect the defenseless, succor the
wounded, receive the dying, and console the anxious and bereaved.
Turn the hearts of our enemies, we beseech Thee, and forgive both
them and us for our share in the sin that has brought this anguish
on mankind; open up to us a way of reconciliation and lead us it the
path of peace; through Jesus Christ, our only Redeemer. Amen.

Army and Navy Service Book 1917

For the Airmen and Others in Hazardous Service

O Almighty God, who sittest on thy throne judging right; We commend to thy fatherly goodness the men serving our Nation at this time of peril (particularly our Airmen and others in hazardous employ) beseeching thee to take into thine own hand both them and the cause which they uphold. Be thou their tower of strength and give them courage in peril and danger. Make them bold through life or death to put their trust in thee, who art the giver of all victory; through Jesus Christ our Lord. Amen.

A Prayer for Those in Training

O Lord, our God, we ask thy help and blessing for all who are now being prepared to take their part in the defense and service of their country. Grant that they may cheerfully perform all necessary duties; preserve them amidst the dangers and temptations which beset them; make them apt and able, that in all things they may quit themselves like men to the honour of their high calling, their country's safety, and thy glory; through him who suffered, died, and rose again for us, thy Son, our Saviour Jesus Christ.

For the Army

O Lord God of Hosts, stretch forth, we pray thee, thine almighty arm to strengthen and protect the soldiers of our country; support them in the day of battle, and in the time of peace keep them safe from all evil; endue them with courage and loyalty; and grant that in all things they may serve without reproach, as seeing thee who art invisible; through Jesus Christ our Lord. Amen.

For the Catholic Church

O Gracious Father, we humbly beseech thee for thy holy catholic Church; that thou wouldst be pleased to fill it with all truth in all peace. Where it is corrupt, purify it; where it is in error, direct it; where in anything it is amiss, reform it; where it is right, strengthen it; where it is in want, provide for it; where it is divided, heal the breaches thereof; for the sake of him who died and rose again, and forever maketh intercession for it, Jesus Christ, thy Son, our Lord. Amen.

Special Prayers in the Face of the Enemy

Thou, O Lord, art just and powerful: O defend our cause against the face of the enemy.

O God, thou art a strong tower of defense to all who fly unto thee: O save us from the violence of the enemy.

O Lord of hosts, fight for us, that we may glorify thee.

O suffer us not to sink under the weight of our sins, or the violence of the enemy.

O Lord arise, help us, and deliver us for thy Name's sake. Amen.

A Prayer When There Appeareth But Small Hope of Recovery

O Father of mercies, and God of all comfort, our only help in time of need; We fly unto thee for succor in behalf of this thy servant, here lying under thy hand in great weakness of body. Look graciously upon him, O Lord; and the more the outward man decayeth, strengthen him, we beseech thee, so much the more continually with thy grace and Holy Spirit in the inner man. Give him unfeigned repentance for all the errors of his life past, and steadfast faith in thy Son Jesus; that his sins may be done away by thy mercy, and his pardon sealed in heaven, before he go hence, and be no more seen.

For the Dying

Almighty God, who willest not that any sinner should die, but rather that he should turn from his wickedness and live; We beseech thee to loose the spirits of those who are dying from every bond and set them free from all evil, that they may rest with all thy saints in the eternal habitations; through Jesus Christ our Lord. Amen.

For Grace to Die

O God, who holdest our souls in life, and hast appointed unto all men once to die; Grant that when our last hour cometh, we may not be dismayed; but may commend our spirits to thy care; trusting in the merits of thy Son our Saviour. And this we beg for the sake of him who died for us that we might live with thee forever. Amen.

A Prayer in Case of Sudden Surprise and Immediate Danger

O Most gracious Father, we fly unto thee for mercy in behalf of this thy servant, here lying under the sudden visitation of thine hand. If it be thy will, preserve his life, that there may be place for repentance; but if thou hast otherwise appointed, let thy mercy supply to him the want of the usual opportunity for the trimming of his lamp. Stir up in him such sorrow for sin, and such fervent love to thee, as may in a short time do the work of many days: that among the praises which thy saints and holy angels shall sing to the honour of thy mercy through eternal ages, it may be to thy unspeakable glory, that thou hast redeemed the soul of this thy servant from eternal death, and made him partaker of the everlasting life, which is through Jesus Christ our Lord. Amen.

Do Not Return Evil for Evil

Lord Jesus Christ, who hast commanded us not to return evil for evil, but to pray for those who hate us; Enable us by thy blessed example and thy loving Spirit, to offer a true prayer for all our enemies (and especially for those persons known to thee who have wrought us harm). If in anything we have given just cause of offence, teach us to feel, and to confess, and to amend our fault, that a way of reconciliation may be found. Deliver them and us from the power of hatred, and may the peace of God rule in all our hearts, both now and evermore. Amen.

For Right Conversation

O God, who hast magnified thy Name and thy Word above all things, fill our hearts with such reverence that we may never take thy holy Name in vain. Purge our thoughts and speech, that no unworthy communications may proceed out of our mouths. Restrain all words that may do hurt, and keep the door of our lips, that we may ever be showing forth thy praise; through Jesus Christ our Lord. Amen.

For Temperance

O God, who didst make man in Thine own image, and hast sanctified our human nature by the Incarnation of thy dear Son; give us grace to keep our bodies in temperance and soberness. Stir up our wills to such abstinence as may safeguard the weak. Deepen our sense of the sinfulness of waste, and of the misery which self indulgence thrusts upon the innocent. Strengthen the efforts to rid our land of drunkenness; and so mightily impel us to avoid all such things as are contrary to our profession, that we may prove ourselves worthy temples of the Holy Ghost; through Jesus Christ our Lord. Amen.

For Acceptable Service

O God, the strength of all those who put their trust in thee; Mercifully accept our prayers; and because , through the weakness of our mortal nature, we can do no good thing without thee, grant us the help of thy grace, that in keeping thy commandments we may please thee, both in will and deed; through Jesus Christ our Lord. Amen.

For Christlikeness

O God, whose blessed Son was manifested that he might destroy the works of all the devil, and make us the sons of God, and heirs of eternal life; Grant us, we beseech thee, that, having this hope, we may purify ourselves, even as he is pure; that, when he shall appear again with power and great glory, we may be made like unto him in his eternal and glorious kingdom; where with thee, O Father, and thee, O Holy Ghost, he liveth and reigneth ever, one God, world without end. Amen.

For Purity

O Lord Jesus Christ, sinless Son of man, who art evermore ready to succor them that are tempted; Grant unto us, thy servants, both valour and constancy, that we may keep evermore undefiled our own purity, fight manfully against the corruption that is in the world, and shield and rescue those that are sore beset. These things we ask of the love of the Father and the power and of the Holy Ghost in thy Name, who with them livest and reignest, one God, world without end. Amen.

For the Love that Blesses

O God, who hast prepared for those who love thee, such, good things as pass man's understanding; Pour into our hearts such love toward thee, that we, loving thee above all things, may obtain thy promises, which exceed all that we can desire; through Jesus Christ our Lord. Amen.

O Lord, we beseech thee, absolve thy people from their offences; that through thy bountiful goodness we may all be delivered from the bands of those sins, which by our frailty we have committed. Grant this O heavenly Father, for Jesus Christ's sake, our blessed Lord and Saviour. Amen.

For Those at Home

Almighty God, Father of our Lord Jesus Christ, of whom the whole family in earth and heaven is named; we commend to thee our loved ones at home. Guard and protect them from all evil. Amid all the separations of this life, keep them and us under thy care and guidance; watch over them and us while we are absent one from the other. Grant us a happy reunion here on earth, and after the separation of this life, unite us all at last in thy heavenly kingdom; through Jesus Christ our Lord. Amen.

Short Prayers Amidst a Storm

Thou, O Lord, who stillest the raging of the sea, hear us, and save us, that we perish not.

O Blessed Saviour, who didst save thy disciples ready to perish in a storm, hear us, and save us, we beseech thee.

Lord, have mercy upon us.
Christ, have mercy upon us.
Lord, have mercy upon us.
O Lord, hear us.
O Christ, hear us.

God the Father, God the son, God the Holy Ghost, have mercy upon us, save us now and evermore. Amen.

The Prayer to be Said Before a Fight at Sea Against any Enemy

O Most powerful and glorious Lord God, the Lord of hosts, that rulest and commandest all things; Thou sittest in the throne judging right, and therefore we make our address to thy Divine Majesty in this our necessity, that thou wouldest take the cause into thine own hand, and judge between us and our enemies. Stir up thy strength, O Lord, and come and help us; for thou givest not always the battle to the strong, but canst save by many or by few. O let not our sins now cry against us for vengeance; but hear us, thy poor servants, begging mercy and imploring thy help, and that thou wouldest be a defense unto us against the face of the enemy. Make it appear that thou art our Saviour and mighty Deliverer, through Jesus Christ our Lord. Amen.

Prayers to be Used in all Ships in Storms at Sea

O Most powerful and glorious Lord God, at whose command the winds blow, and lift up the waves of the sea, and who stillest the rage thereof; We, thy creatures, but miserable sinners, do in this our great distress cry unto thee for help; Save, Lord, or else we perish. We confess, when we have been safe, and seen all things quiet about us, we have forgotten thee our God, and refused to hearken to the still voice of thy word, and to obey thy commandments: but now we see how terrible thou art in all thy works of wonder, the great God to be feared above all: and therefore we adore thy Divine Majesty, acknowledging thy power, and imploring thy goodness. Help, Lord, and save us for thy mercy's sake in Jesus Christ, thy Son our Lord. Amen.

A Thanksgiving for an Escape from Peril

O Lord God, in whose hand is the life of everything, and the breath of all mankind; We magnify thy goodness in that thou hast been pleased to save from deadly hurt thy servant who now desireth (or for whom we desire) to offer thee the sacrifice of praise and thanksgiving. Give him grace, we humbly beseech thee, worthily to spend in thy service the days which thou hast so mercifully prolonged, that henceforth dwelling always under thy protection he may abide in thy love unto his life's end; through Jesus Christ our Saviour. Amen.

Thanksgivings

To my prayers, O Lord, I join my unfeigned thanks for all thy mercies; for my being, my reason, and all other endowments and faculties of soul and body; for my health, friends, food, and raiment, and all the other comforts and conveniences of life. Above all, I adore thy mercy in sending thy only Son into the world, to redeem me from sin and eternal death, and in giving me the knowledge and sense of my duty towards thee. I bless thee for thy patience with me, notwithstanding my many and great provocations; for all the directions, assistances, and comforts of thy Holy Spirit; for thy continual care and watchful providence over me through the whole course of my life; and particularly for the mercies and benefits of the past day; beseeching thee to continue these thy blessings to me, and to give me grace to show my thankfulness in a sincere obedience to his laws, through whose merits and intercession I received them all, thy Son our Saviour Jesus Christ. Amen.

O Almighty God, the Sovereign Commander of all the world, in whose hand is power and might, which none is able to withstand; We bless and magnify thy great and glorious Name for this happy Victory, the whole glory whereof we do ascribe to thee, who art the only giver of victory. And, we beseech thee, give us grace to improve this great mercy to thy glory, the advancement of thy Gospel, the honour of our country, and, as much as in us lieth, to the good of all mankind. And, we beseech thee, give us such a sense of this great mercy, as may engage us to a true thankfulness, such as may appear in our lives by an humble, holy and obedient walking before thee all our days; through Jesus Christ our Lord, to whom, with thee and the Holy Spirit, as for all thy mercies, so in particular for this Victory and Deliverance, be all glory and honour, world without end. Amen.

A Thanksgiving for the Beginning of a Recovery

Great and mighty God, who bringest down to the grave, and
bringest up again; we bless thy wonderful goodness, for having
turned our heaviness into joy and our mourning into gladness,
by restoring this our brother to some degree of his former health.
Blessed be thy Name that thou didst not forsake him in his sickness;
but didst visit him with comforts from above; didst support him
in patience and submission to thy will; and at last didst send him
seasonable relief. Perfect, we beseech thee, this thy mercy towards
him; and prosper the means which shall be made use of for his
cure: that, being restored to health of body, vigour of mind, and
cheerfulness of spirit, he may be able to go to thine house, to offer
thee an oblation with great gladness, and to bless thy holy Name for
all thy goodness towards him; through Jesus Christ our Saviour, to
whom, with thee and the Holy Spirit, be all honour and glory, world
without end. Amen.

For A Person Under Affliction

O Merciful God, and heavenly Father, who hast taught us in thy
holy Word that thou dost not willingly afflict or grieve the children
of men; Look with pity, we beseech thee, upon the sorrows of thy
servants, for whom our prayers are desired. In thy wisdom thou
hast seen fit to visit him with trouble, and to bring distress upon
him. Remember him, O Lord, in mercy; sanctify thy fatherly
correction to him; endue his soul with patience under his affliction,
and with resignation to thy blessed will; comfort him with a sense of
thy goodness; lift up thy countenance upon him, and give him peace;
through Jesus Christ our Lord. Amen.

For the Marine Corps

Eternal and loving Father, we commend to thy protection and care the officers and men of our Marine Corps. Guide and direct them in the maintenance of our country's honour. Protect them in the hour of danger. Grant that wherever they serve our Nation—on land or sea, they may at all times put their trust in thee, and commit themselves and their loved ones to thy fatherly keeping, until they are finally called into thy haven of rest and peace; through Jesus Christ our Lord. Amen.

For the Navy

O Eternal Lord God, who alone spreadest out the heavens, and rulest the raging of the sea; Vouchsafe to take into thy almighty and most gracious protection our country's Navy, and all who serve therein. Preserve them from the dangers of the sea, and from the violence of the enemy; that they may be a safeguard unto the United States of America, and a security for such as pass on the seas upon their lawful occasions; that the inhabitants of our land may in peace and quietness serve thee our God; to the glory of thy Name, through Jesus Christ our Lord. Amen.

A Prayer of Protection

God of all comfort, who didst sustain Thy blessed Son when he was bound and scourged, and didst send an angel to deliver Thine apostle from imprisonment, mercifully befriend all prisoners and captives. Defend them from injustice and cruelty; uplift them by the angel of Thy presence; and in Thy good time restore them to liberty and glad service of Thee and their country. For the sake of him who through suffering and death had redeemed us, Jesus Christ our Lord. Amen.

A Prayer for Persons Troubled in Mind or in Conscience

O Blessed Lord, the Father of mercies, and the God of all comfort; We beseech thee, look down in pity and compassion upon this thy afflicted servant. Thou writest bitter things against him, and makest him to possess his former iniquities; thy wrath lieth hard upon him, and his soul is full of trouble. But, O merciful God, who hast written thy holy Word for our learning, that we, through patience and comfort of thy holy Scriptures, might have hope; give him a right understanding of himself, and of thy threats and promises; that he may neither cast away his confidence in thee, nor place it anywhere but in thee. Give him strength against all his temptations, and heal all his distempers. Break not the bruised reed, nor quench the smoking flax. Shut not up thy tender mercies in displeasure; but make him to hear of joy and gladness, that the bones with thou hast broken may rejoice. Deliver him from fear of the enemy, and lift up the light of thy countenance upon him, and give him peace, through the merits and mediation of Jesus Christ our Lord. Amen.

For the Dead

Incline, O Lord, Thine ear to our prayers, and of Thy mercy bring Thy servants who have died in battle from their wounds into the place of peace and light and admit them to the fellowship of the blessed ones who have laid down their lives for their friends; through Jesus Christ our Lord. Amen.

In Pain

Help us, God of our life, to bear our pain as thy beloved Son
bore his trials and passion, so that we may gather strength out of
weakness and suffering, and consecrate our sorrows even as he did.
Enable us to bear quietly whatever hardness there may be in our
lot, neither exulting in our pride, nor yielding to despondency, but
always relying upon thee. And be pleased, O thou great Deliverer,
to put an end at last to our suffering, whether in tranquil life, or at
the coming of the final peace; and when thou callest us to give an
account of our stewardship of pain, may we be found worthy of the
recompense of those whose suffering was instead of work for thee.
Amen.

For Our Country

Almighty God, who hast given us this good land for our heritage;
we humbly beseech thee that we may always prove ourselves a
people mindful of thy favour, glad to do thy will. Bless our land
with honourable industry, sound learning, and pure manners. Save
us from violence, discord and confusion; from pride and arrogancy,
and from every evil way. Defend our liberties; preserve our unity;
fashion into one happy people the multitudes brought hither out of
many kindreds and tongues. Endue with the spirit of wisdom those
to whom in thy Name we entrust the authority of government, to
the end that there be justice and peace at home, and that through
obedience to thy law we show forth thy praise among the nations of
the earth. In the time of prosperity fill our hearts with thankfulness,
and in the day of trouble suffer not our trust in thee to fail; through
Jesus Christ our Lord. Amen.

Washington's Prayer

Almighty God; We make our earnest prayer that thou wilt keep the United States in thy holy protection; that thou wilt incline the hearts of the citizens to cultivate a spirit of subordination and obedience to government; and entertain a brotherly affection and love for one another and for their fellow citizens of the United States at large. And finally that thou wilt most graciously be pleased to dispose us all to do justice, to love mercy and to demean ourselves with that charity, humility and pacific temper of mind which were the characteristics of the divine author of our blessed religion, and without a humble imitation of whose example in these things we can never hope to be a happy nation. Grant our supplication, we beseech thee, through Jesus Christ our Lord. Amen.

For Victory

O Lord God of Hosts, strengthen and guide this Nation and our Allies, that we may labour with valour for the establishment on earth of thy reign of law and love, of freedom and righteousness, and crown our endeavours with speedy victory and lasting peace; through Jesus Christ our Lord. Amen.

A Prayer Book for Soldiers and Sailors 1917

A Prayer of Strength for the Ministering

O Merciful God, whose blessed Son went about doing good; Uphold with thy strength and grace those who do service to the wounded and the sick; grant to the ministers of thy gospel faithfulness and love, to the physicians and surgeons wisdom and skill, to the nurses sympathy and patience; and we beseech thee to protect and bless them in all dangers, anxieties, and labours; through Jesus Christ our Lord. Amen.

A Prayer Book for Soldiers and Sailors 1917 &
The West Point Prayer Book 1948

1918

Thanksgiving After Victory

O Almighty God, the Sovereign Commander of all the world, in whose hand is power and might, which none is able to withstand; We bless and magnify thy great and glorious Name for this happy Victory, the whole glory whereof we do ascribe to thee, who art the only giver of victory. And, we beseech thee, give us grace to improve this great mercy to thy glory, the advancement of thy Gospel, the honour of our country, and, as much as in us lieth, to the good of all mankind. And, we beseech thee, give us such a sense of this great mercy, as may engage us to a true thankfulness, such as may appear in our lives by an humble, holy and obedient walking before thee all our days; through Jesus Christ our Lord; to whom, with thee and the Holy Spirit, as for all thy mercies, so in particular for this Victory and Deliverance, be all glory and honour, world without end. Amen.

The Campaign Prayer Book 1918

I Need Thee Every Hour
Annie S. Hawks (1872)

I need thee every hour, most gracious Lord;
no tender voice like thine can peace afford.

Refrain: I need thee, O I need thee; every hour I need thee;
O bless me now, my Savior, I come to thee.

I need thee every hour; stay thou nearby;
temptations lose their power when thou art nigh.

I need thee every hour, most Holy One;
O make me thine indeed, thou blessed Son.

1920

Thanks for Our Country

O God of purity and peace, God of light and freedom, God of comfort and joy, we thank thee for our country, this great land of hope, whose wide doors thou hast opened to so many millions that struggle with hardship and with hunger in the crowded Old World.

We give thanks to the power that has made and preserved us a nation, that has carried our ship of state through storm and darkness and has given us a place of honor and power that we might bear aloft the standard of impartial liberty and impartial law.

May our altars and our schools ever stand as pillars of welfare; may the broad land be filled with homes of intelligent and contented industry, that through the long generations our land may be a happy land and our country a power of good will among nations. Amen.

Charles Gordon Ames

My Desire

Heavenly Father, thou knowest I desire to do my whole duty now and always. Give me an open mind to hear thy call and a willing heart to respond. May I be able through thee both to do and to dare. Keep me from faltering or turning aside from any task thou hast given me. May I be strong, having on the whole armor of God, and on every battlefield may I acquit myself like a true soldier of the Cross. Amen.

Judson Swift

Christmas Service Invocation

O God, of heaven glory, and source of earthly peace and good will; may our Christmas be merry, because it is touched with joy divine; may the remembrance of thy Christ's birth be holy, because he is really born in our hearts today, in his purity and love; through the same, thy son, Jesus Christ our Lord. Amen.

A Prayer for a Soldier's Mother

Lord Jesus, thou hast known
A mother's love and tender care,
And thou wilt hear while for my own mother most dear
I make this Sabbath prayer.
Protect her life, I pray,
Who gave the gift of life to me;
And may she know, from day to day, the deepening glow
Of joy that comes from thee.
I cannot pay my debt
For all the love that she has given;
But thou, love's Lord, wilt not forget her due reward,--
Bless her in earth and heaven.

Henry Van Dyke
*Professor of English at Princeton University and appointed Minister to the
Netherlands and Luxembourg by President Woodrow Wilson.*

He Who Gives All Things

Father of mankind, who givest to thy creatures all things richly to
enjoy! What can we render thee for all the abounding blessings that
crown our lives! What canst thou do but give, what can we do but
receive, since all we can offer is already thine own. Thou hast given
the earth to the children of men. We give thanks and praise for the
coming and going of day and night, for the march of the seasons, for
the ever repeated miracle of growth by which all creatures are fed.
We give thanks for the countless common benefits and comforts of
every day and night: for the flowers of human kindness that spring
along the path; for the law of commandments which teaches that we
are thy servants; for the gospel of love which assures us that we are
thy children. Amen.

The Army and Navy Hymnal 1920

1940

For Safety

We humbly beseech Thee, O Father, mercifully to look upon our infirmities and, for the glory of Thy name, turn from us all those evils that we most justly have deserved; and grant that in all our troubles we may put our whole trust and confidence in Thy mercy, and evermore serve Thee in holiness and pureness of living, to Thy honor and glory; through our only Mediator and Advocate Jesus Christ our Lord. Amen.

Help Me to Choose, O Lord

Help me to choose, O Lord, from out of the maze
And multitude of things that by me roll,
One thing to work, and pray for here on earth —
Something to keep before me as a goal;
That when I die my days may form for Thee,
Not fragments, but one perfect whole.
I seek, O Lord, some purpose in my life,
Some end which will my daily acts control,
So many days seem wasted now to see —
All disconnected hours that by me roll.
Help me to choose, O Lord, while I am young,
Something to keep before me as a goal.

Marjorie Hillis

Make Our Lives Purposeful

And now, O Lord, we come to Thee in days when swift tragedy abounds, when worlds are shaking as before coming judgments, when civilization itself is tottering, when in the balances of God so many are being weighted and found wanting, when the realities which make life worth living are facing quick destruction—

Make our lives real and purposeful, rich and pure and good. Cleanse from us all that is sordid and mean, low and impure, all that is displeasing to Thee. Give us great ambition sanctified by dedication to Thee. Help us to choose aright a life full of blessing to ourselves and our fellows. Set us on fire by Thy Spirit so that we may fire others with Thy truth. Help us to right the wrong, make straight the crooked paths. Make us in all we do to follow Thy Son Jesus Christ and to bring others to follow Him. Be merciful to us; save us and all the world.

Seal our purpose, O Lord, with Thy benediction and give us new birth and a holy desire, in all we do, to please only Thee. For we know that to us has come the choice of eternal destinies. Lead us to choose aright,--through Jesus Christ our Lord.

Service Prayer Book, 1940

Nearer, My God, to Thee
Sarah F. Adams (1841)

Nearer, my God, to Thee, nearer to Thee!
E'en though it be a cross that raiseth me,
Still all my song shall be, nearer, my God, to Thee.

    Refrain:
    Nearer, my God, to Thee,
    Nearer to Thee!

There in my Father's home, safe and at rest,
There in my Savior's love, perfectly blest;
Age after age to be, nearer my God to Thee.

1941

A Prayer for Loved Ones

O God, the Protector and Helper of all thy children, the Comfort and the Stay of the solitary, and those who are separated from those they love, we commit unto Thee and thy fatherly keeping our loved ones, beseeching Thee to grant unto them every good gift for the body and the soul, and to unite us all, present and absent in true faith and love. Through Jesus Christ our Lord. Amen.

Gladness and Peace

Grant us, O Lord, to pass this day in gladness and peace, without stumbling and without stain; that, reaching the eventide victorious over all temptation we may praise Thee, the Eternal God, who art blessed forever, and doest hold in they hand the destinies of the visible creation, world without end. Through Christ our Lord. Amen.

A Prayer for Support

O Lord, support us all the day long of this troublous life, until the shadows lengthen and the evening comes and the busy world is hushed and the fever of life is over, and our work is done. Then of Thy mercy grant us a safe lodging, a holy rest and peace at the last, through Jesus Christ our Lord. Amen

A Prayer at Taps

Before we go to rest we commit ourselves to thy care, O God our Father, beseeching Thee through Christ our Lord to keep alive Thy grace in our hearts. Watch Thou, O Heavenly Father, with those who wake, or watch, or weep tonight, and give Thine angels charge over those who sleep. Tend those who are sick, rest those who are weary, sooth those who suffer, pity those in affliction; be near and bless those who are dying, and keep under Thy holy care those who are dear to us. Through Christ our Lord. Amen.

Song and Service Book for Ship and Field, 1941

Be My Support, O God

O God, keep my tongue from evil and my lips from speaking guile. Be my support when grief silences my voice, and my comfort when woe bends my spirit. Implant humility in my soul, and strengthen my heart with perfect faith in Thee. Help me to be strong in temptation and trial and to be patient and forgiving when others wrong me. Guide me by the light of Thy counsel, that I may ever find strength in Thee, my Rock and my Redeemer. Amen.

Abridged Prayer Book for Jews in the
Armed Forces of the United States, 1941

Sweet Hour of Prayer
William Walford (1845)

Sweet hour of prayer! sweet hour of prayer!
That calls me from a world of care,
And bids me at my Father's throne
Make all my wants and wishes known.
In seasons of distress and grief,
My soul has often found relief
And oft escaped the tempter's snare
By thy return, sweet hour of prayer!

1942

For World Peace

O Almighty God, who makest even the wrath of man to turn to thy praise; We beseech thee so to order and dispose the issue of this war that we may be brought through strife to a lasting peace, and that the nations of the world may be united in a firmer fellowship, for the promotion of thy glory and the good of all mankind; through Jesus Christ our Lord. Amen.

Prayer Book for Soldiers and Sailors, 1942

Dealing with Criticism

Teach us, O God, to deal wisely, patiently and constructively with our critics and opponents. Help us to love them even though they do not love us. May we understand the real and deeper needs that lie beneath all the storms of controversy, and may we ever seek, not personal vindication, but deeper insights into truth. Deliver us from blind partisanship, and keep us close to Jesus Christ our Lord. In His name. Amen.

Lead Us Away from Temptation

O God, we come to thee with no false sense of our own importance or perfection. We come only as those who remember that "Still stands thine ancient sacrifice, an humble and a contrite heart." Lead us away from the temptations which might overwhelm us and deliver us from the evil which might break down the inner citadel and sanctuary of our lives. Through Jesus Christ, our Saviour. Amen.

Fighting for Peace and Salvation

Dear Father of peace, prepare our hearts to fight for the peace and salvation of the world. Grant that by thy help we may put on the whole spiritual armor and battle for righteousness in this world of sin. We ask in Jesus' name. Amen.

Rations 100 Days, 1942

Blessed Assurance
Fanny J. Crosby (1873)

Blessed assurance, Jesus is mine!
O what a foretaste of glory divine!
Heir of salvation, purchase of God,
Born of His Spirit, washed in His blood.

> Refrain:
> This is my story, this is my song,
> praising my Savior all the day long;
> this is my story, this is my song,
> praising my Savior all the day long.

Perfect submission, perfect delight!
Visions of rapture now burst on my sight;
Angels descending bring from above
Echoes of mercy, whispers of love.

Perfect submission, all is at rest!
I in my Savior am happy and blest,
Watching and waiting, looking above,
Filled with his goodness, lost in His love.

1943

For All Airmen

Most High God, who ridest upon the wings of the wind and makest the clouds thy chariots: We commit to thine especial care the airmen of our flying force. Give them a clear eye and a cool mind; nerve them to meet confidently the times of their swift and solitary trial; protect them in brief moments of sudden peril; and if need be, steel their spirits to meet death unafraid. Grant that through all vicissitudes their spirits may mount up on wings like eagles; vouchsafe to them in the exercise of their newest skills and the gallant and generous soul of chivalry; and in thy good providence return them to the ways of the earth with the secrets of an upper air. Amen

Bless Our Native Land

Lord, bless our native land; in peace so preserve it that it corrupt not; in war so defend it that it suffer not; in plenty so order it that it riot not; in want so moderate it that it may wait patiently for thee.

> Prayers for Private Devotions in War-Time,
> Harvard University, 1943

Prayer for Victory

O God of battles, Who grantest the victory to those who put their trust in Thee: mercifully hear the prayers of us, Thy servants, that the evil designs of our enemies being defeated, we may praise Thee with unceasing gratitude. Through Christ our Lord. Amen.

A Prayer for Soldiers

My Lord Jesus Christ strengthen me in the company of the Church Militant. Help me to be strong in faith and brave in battle. Help my companions that they also may be good soldiers and always worth of their pledge of devotion to God and our country. Give courage and comfort to all our dear ones at home from whom we must be separated for a time. Grant that when this war is ended we may safely return to them and give Thee thanks for all Thy services. Who livest and reignest, world without end. Amen.

Prayer Book for Catholic Servicemen, 1943

What a Friend We Have in Jesus
Joseph Scriven (1855)

What a Friend we have in Jesus, all
our sins and griefs to bear!
What a privilege to carry everything
to God in prayer!
O what peace we often forfeit, O
what needless pain we bear,
All because we do not carry
everything to God in prayer.

Blessed Savior, Thou hast promised
Thou wilt all our burdens bear
May we ever, Lord, be bringing all
to Thee in earnest prayer.
Soon in glory bright unclouded there
will be no need for prayer
Rapture, praise and endless worship
will be our sweet portion there.

1944

Help Me to Do My Duty

O God, most merciful and just, look upon this suppliant soldier and help me to do my duty in all things for love of Thee. Make me strong in conflict, brave in adversity, and patient in suffering. Make me vigilant to defend my country against her enemies and proud to carry her cause fearlessly into battle. I do not ask to be preserved free from all bodily harm, and if death is the price I must pay for my country's freedom, I will pay it gladly, trusting in Thy infinite mercy that Thou wilt make a place for me in heaven, there to know peace and happiness for all eternity. Bless and protect my peace and happiness for all eternity. Bless and protect my loved ones at home, and grant that my sacrifices on the field of battle may make me worthy of their trust and confidence, through Christ our Lord. Amen.

Brigadier General La Vern G. Saunders
Twentieth Bomber Command, United States Army

Prayer of a Fighter Pilot*

O God, My Father, The Great Referee of earth and sea and sky, be with me in combat and adversity. Strengthen my love for the land that has given me birth and make me worthy of the sacrifices of my fathers in hewing America from the wilderness they found. Endow me with the courage to face danger in spite of fear. Make me resolve that the blood of my fathers was not shed in vain and that regardless of cost—our way of life shall endure. Keep me physically strong that I may better defend my home and my native land. Keep me mentally awake that my enemies may never again strike with surprise and deal with me in treachery. Uplift my morals that I may better maintain the honor of my country and the reverence of my forefathers. Let duty to God and Country be my most sublime aspirations, and kindle my heart and soul with the determination to die rather than yield the ideals of my world. O God, My Father, whatever duty befalls me when my country calls, may I acquit myself as worthy of Thy Guidance.

And when my combat's over and my flying days are done I will store my ship forever in the airdrome of the sun. Then I'll meet the Referee, Great God, my Flying Boss, Whose Wingspread fills the heavens from Polaris to the Cross....Amen.

Brigadier General Robert L. Scott, Jr.
Fighter Pilot, United States Army Air Forces.
Author of God is My Co-Pilot.

From General Eisenhower

Almighty God, we are about to be committed to a task from which some of us will not return. We go willing to this hazardous adventure because we believe that those concepts of human dignity rights and justice that Your Son expounded to the world, and which are represented in the government of our beloved country, are in peril of extinction from the earth. We are ready to sacrifice ourselves for our country and our God. We do not ask, individually, for our safe return. But we earnestly pray that You will help each of us to do his full duty. Permit none of us to fail a comrade in the fight. Above all, sustain us in our conviction in the justice and righteousness of our cause so that we may rise above all terror of the enemy and come to You, if called, in the humble pride of the good soldier and in the certainty of Your infinite mercy. Amen.

General Dwight D. Eisenhower
United States Army
Supreme Commander of American-British Forces in Europe

Strengthen Us with Courage

Eternal God, whose ways are perfect and whose life is unfailing, help us in these difficult days to realize our need of the guidance and strength Thou alone canst give. Too many times our sense of self-reliance has robbed us of Thy divine help. We live in troublous times, and dangers are many. We pray now that thou wilt make us adequate for all that life may bring us. Save us from that inner weakness of spirit which would cause us to fail. More and more strengthen us with ennobling courage, great faith and the will to see life through. We pray in the name of Jesus Christ, our Lord. Amen.

Chaplain (Commander) C. H. Lambdin
Dean of Chaplains School, College of William and Mary

In the Midst of Dangers

O God, who knowest us to be set in the midst of so many and great dangers, that by reason of the frailty of our nature we cannot always stand upright; grant to us such strength and protection as may support us in all dangers and carry us through all temptations; through Jesus Christ our Lord.

The Book of Common Prayer

Christ before us. Christ in us. Christ over us.

May the strength of God pilot us. May the power of God preserve us. May the wisdom of God instruct us. May the hand of God protect us. May the way of God direct us. May the shield of God defend us.

May the host of God guard us against the snares of the Evil One and the temptations of the world.

May Christ be with us. Christ before us. Christ in us. Christ over us. May Thy salvation, O Lord, be always ours this day and for evermore. Amen.

St. Patrick

For Peace

Almighty God, our heavenly Father, guide, we beseech thee, the Nations of the world into the way of justice and truth, and establish among them the peace which is the fruit of righteousness, that they may become the Kingdom of our Lord and Saviour Jesus Christ. Amen.

The Book of Common Prayer

The President's Prayer

God of the free, we pledge our hearts and lives today to the
cause of all free mankind. Grant us victory over the tyrants who
would enslave all free men and nations. Grant us brotherhood
in hope and union, to come which shall and must unite all the
children of earth….We are all of us children of earth—grant us
that simple knowledge. If our brothers are oppressed, then we
are oppressed. If they hunger, we hunger. If their freedom is
taken away, our freedom is not secure. Grant us a common faith
that man shall know bread and peace—that he shall know justice
and righteousness, freedom and security, and equal opportunity
and an equal chance to do his best, not only in our own lands, but
throughout the world. And in the faith let us march, toward the
clean world our hands can make. Amen.

Read before the nation by Franklin Delano Roosevelt
Commander in Chief of the Army and Navy of the United States
This prayer was read by the President on Flag Day, June 14, 1942.
It was composed for the occasion by Stephen Vincent Benet.

For the Maintenance of Our Liberties

O Eternal God, through whose mighty power our fathers won their
liberties of old; grant, we beseech thee, that we and all the people of
this land may have grace to maintain these liberties in righteousness
and peace; through Jesus Christ our Lord. Amen

                              The Book of Common Prayer

Give Us Victory

Almighty God, our Heavenly Father, Thou art always with thy children. Through the power of Thy Spirit make us ever conscious of Thy nearness, and in the confidence gained thereby, enable us this day to say and do only that which is according to Thy holy will. May we be possessed of that peace which Thou alone canst give. In danger, give us courage through the assurance of Thy protection. In service may we be enduring peace that Thy Kingdom may come and Thy Will be fully accomplished throughout the whole world. This, with the forgiveness of our sins, we ask through Jesus Christ, Our Lord. Amen.

Chaplain (Colonel) J. Burt Webster, D.D.
Chief of Chaplains, Second Service Command,
United States Army

Love

Almighty God, our Father, we lift our hearts in prayer to Thee now in behalf of those whose lives have been shadowed by war. All over Thy world there are those whose hopes and homes have felt the distress of the days in which we live. Many of us have come to see what a majestic thing love is for the first time in our lives. Our love for others has never seemed so real. It crosses oceans and nations afar. Day and night those we are devoted to stand before us in fine memory and affection. And if our love for one another is so real, may we also realize that Thy great love toward us is even stronger. Lead us straight into the living consciousness of Thy love, which is always greater than our own. We pray in the name and spirit of Jesus Christ our Lord. Amen.

Chaplain (Commander) C. H. Lambdin
United States Navy
Dean of Chaplains School, College of William and Mary

Thy Blessing Upon the United States Marine Corps

We invoke Thy Blessing, O God, upon the United States Marine Corps. Breathe Thou into the heart and soul of every Marine Thy Spirit that he may live a life of consecration and devotion to the highest ideals as he finds himself on the battle fields of democracy. Save him from softness of body and soul. Fill him with firmness and zeal, stamina and purpose. May he set up his banner, wherever his footsteps fall, in Thy Name, for liberty, for fraternity, for equality! Make us all fit to represent Thy Will as we catch the spirit of the Marine. O God, speak steadiness to our spirits this hour — that we may carry on. Amen.

Chaplain (Captain) M. M. Witherspoon
United States Navy

Prayer for Our Friends and Families

O Lord, our Heavenly Father, who hast bestowed upon us the blessings of friends and families, look down in love upon our kindred. Protect and keep them from all harm; prosper and bless them in all things good; suffer them never to be lonely, unhappy nor troubled; let no shadow come between them and us to divide our hearts; and in Thine own good time bring us home to them again. Through the same Thy Son Jesus Christ our Lord. Amen.

From the prayers used at the church service held Sunday morning, August 10, 1941, aboard H.M.S. Prince of Wales, attended by Franklin D. Roosevelt, President of the United States, and Winston S. Churchill, Prime Minister of Great Britain.

For Those We Love

Almighty God, we entrust all who are dear to us to thy never-failing care and love, for this life and the life to come; knowing that thou art doing for them better things than we can desire or pray for; through Jesus Christ our Lord.   Amen.

The Book of Common Prayer

A Prayer for Her

Lord, give her strength when she is weak
And peace when troubled is her heart;
Lord, send her hope when hope is gone,
And courage when her battles start.
There's only one thing more I ask —
You'll understand I know, so please,
Lord bless her while she waits alone,
And give her faith for times like these… Amen

Dorothy M. Ballenger, A Navy Wife
Her husband is Earl L. Ballenger,
Boatswain's Mate First Class, United States Navy
From Our Navy Magazine

For Those Who Have Given Their Lives

Almighty god, our heavenly Father, in whose hands are the living and the dead; We give thee thanks for all those thy servants who have laid down their lives in the service of our country. Grant to them thy mercy and the light of thy presence, that the good work which thou hast begun in them may be perfected; through Jesus Christ thy Son our Lord. Amen.

The Book of Common Prayer

For Departing Battalions

Almighty God, our heavenly Father, send down upon this battalion Thy richest gifts, that they who serve therein may be harmed by no adversity either physical or spiritual; endow its officers with wisdom, zeal, and patience; inspire its men with the spirit of truth, courage, and loyalty; and enable all to maintain the honor of the Navy unsullied. Strengthen and increase their admiration for honest dealings and clean thinking, so that they may hate that which is evil and love that which is good. Guard them against irreverence in the sacred things of life. Fill their hearts with the spirit of comradeship, so that they may know sympathy for those who suffer. Hasten, O god, our victory that these, Thy servants, may soon return to their families and loved ones and this troubled world may be at peace. May the grace of the Lord Jesus Christ, and the love of God, and the communion of the Holy Ghost be with you now and forever more. Amen.

Prayers of the United States Navy

For the Navy

O Eternal Lord God, who alone spreadest out the heavens, and rulest the raging of the sea; Vouchsafe to take into thy almighty and most gracious protection our country's Navy, and all who serve therein. Preserve them from the dangers of the sea, and from the violence of the enemy; that they may be a safeguard unto the United States of America, and a security for such as pass on the seas upon their lawful occasions; that the inhabitants of our land may in peace and quietness serve thee our God, to the glory of thy Name; through Jesus Christ our Lord. Amen.

The Book of Common Prayer

Missing in Action

Almighty God, Father of all mankind, whose love reaches all men everywhere, we pray Thee for all Thy servants reported missing in action in this war for human liberty. Thou knowest where they are and in what state of body and soul they may be. In Thy infinite love be with them (especially Thy servant, ------------) [sic], comfort and strengthen them and, if it by Thy Holy Will, restore them to us. Grant to them and to us Thy peace which passes human understanding; through Jesus Christ our Lord. Amen.

Chaplain (Lieutenant Colonel) Henry Darlington

A Prayer from the Commandant of the United States Marine Corps*

O Almighty God, who art a strong tower of defense unto thy servants against the face of their enemies: We yield thee praise and thanksgiving for our deliverance from those great and apparent dangers wherewith we were compassed. We acknowledged it thy goodness that we were not delivered over as a prey unto them; beseeching thee still to continue such thy mercies towards us, that all the world may know that thou art our Saviour and mighty deliverer; through Jesus Christ our Lord. Amen.

Contributed to this volume as his favorite prayer by
Lieutenant General Alexander A. Vandergrift
Commandant, United States Marine Corps
From The Book of Common Prayer

In Times of Anguish

I pray that our Heavenly Father may assuage the anguish of your bereavement and leave you only the cherished memory of the loved and lost, and the solemn pride that must be yours to have laid so costly a sacrifice upon the altar of freedom.

Abraham Lincoln
Letter to a mother whose five sons were killed in action

For Fallen Comrades

O God, we pray Thee that the memory of our comrades fallen in battle may be ever sacred in our hearts; that the sacrifice which they have offered for our country's cause may be acceptable in Thy sight; and that an entrance into Thine eternal peace may, by Thy pardoning Grace, be open unto them through Jesus Christ our Lord and Saviour. Amen.

> Contributed to this volume as his favorite prayer by Admiral Ernest J. King, Commander in Chief of the United States Fleet and Chief of Naval Operations

A Prayer for Strength in Sickness

O God, our Refuge in pain, our Strength in weakness, our Help in trouble, we come to Thee in our hour of need, beseeching Thee to have mercy upon this Thine afflicted servant. O loving Father, relieve his pain. Yet if he needs must suffer, strengthen him, that he may bear his sufferings with patience and as his day is, so may his strength be. Let not his heart be troubled, but shed down upon him the peace which passeth understanding. Though now for a season, if need be, he is in heaviness through his manifold trials, yet comfort him, O Lord, in all his sorrows, and let his mourning be turned into joy, and his sickness into health; through Jesus Christ our only Lord and Saviour. Amen.

> Anonymous

A Prayer of Gratitude and Protection

Eddie Rickenbacker and two companions were rescued from a rubber raft after twenty-one days at sea. Their initial food supply was four oranges. "Frankly and humbly," says Rickenbacker, "we prayed for our deliverance. Within an hour after our prayers, a seagull landed on my head. That seagull kept us alive."

O Lord, I thank thee for the strength and blessings thou hast given me, and even though I have walked through the valley of the shadow of death, I feared no evil, for thy rod and thy staff comforted me event unto the four corners of the world. I have sinned, O Lord, but through thy mercy thou hast shown me the light of thy saving grace.

In thy care we are entrusting our boys and girls in the Services scattered throughout the entire world, and we know that in thee they are finding their haven of hope. Be with our leaders, O Lord; give them wisdom to lead until that day, be with those at home—strengthen them for whatever may lie ahead. Be with our enemies, O Lord, and through the light of thy divine grace, may they reconsecrate themselves to thy service as we are reconsecrating ourselves, so all peoples of the world will sign in unison "Glory to God in the Highest," as only through thee can we realize our hopes for peace everlasting. In Jesus' name I ask it. Amen.

Captain Eddie Rickenbacker
Aboard H.M.S Prince of Wales, at Sea

For Those Suffering in War

Let us pray for all who suffer by reason of the War, for the sick and wounded, for prisoners, for the exiled and homeless, for the anxious and bereaved. We bring before Thee, O Lord, the griefs and perils of peoples and nations; the sighing of prisoners; the necessities of the homeless, and helplessness of the weak; the pains of the sick and wounded; the sorrows of the bereaved. Comfort and relieve them, O Merciful Father, according to their several needs, for the sake of Thy Son, our Saviour and Christ. Amen.

O God, the righteous Judge strong and patient, who by the words and wounds of Thy dear Son has bidden us pray for them that despitefully use us; we beseech Thee so to turn the hearts of our enemies that, when this tyranny be overpast, the divisions of all peoples may be healed, in the bond and by the blessing of the same, our Lord and Saviour Jesus Christ. Amen.

From the prayers used at the church service held Sunday morning, August 10, 1941, aboard H.M.S Prince of Wales, attended by Franklin D. Roosevelt, President of the United States, and Winston S. Churchill, Prime Minister of Great Britain.

Atlantic Charter Meeting

Let Us Unite

Let us unite in imploring the Supreme Ruler of Nations to spread His holy protection over these United States to turn the machinations of the wicked, to the confirming of our Constitution; to enable us at all times to root out internal sedition and put invasion to flight; to perpetuate to our country that prosperity which His goodness has already conferred; and to verify the anticipations for this government begin a safeguard of human rights. Amen.

George Washington

Keep Me From Bitterness

Keep me from bitterness. It is so easy
To nurse sharp bitter thoughts each dull dark hour!
Against self-pity, Man of sorrows, defend me,
With Thy deep sweetness and Thy gentle power.
And out of all this hurt of pain and heartbreak
Help me to harvest a new sympathy
For suffering human kind, a wiser pity
For those who lift a heavier cross with Thee…
Amen.

O God, Inspire Us to Cheerfulness

O God, animate us to cheerfulness. May we have the bright
circumstances of our lot, and maintain a perpetual contentedness
under Thy allotments. Fortify us from despondency, from yielding
to dejection. Teach us that no evil is intolerable but a guilty
conscience, and that nothing can hurt us, if, with true loyalty of
affection, we keep Thy commandments and take refuge in Thee;
through Jesus Christ our Lord. Amen.

William Ellery Channing

George Washington's Prayer for the United States

Almighty God, we make our earnest prayer that Thou wilt keep
the United States in Thy holy protection; that Thou wilt incline
the hearts of the citizens to cultivate a spirit of subordination and
obedience to government; to entertain a brotherly affection and love
for one another and for their fellow-citizens of the United States at
large. Amen.

George Washington
Prayer after his Inauguration

For Untroubled Sleep

O God, Who hast drawn over weary day the restful veil of night, enfold us in Thy heavenly peace. Lift from our hands our tasks, and all through the night carry in Thy care the full weight of our burdens and sorrows; that in untroubled slumber we may press our weariness close to Thy strength, and win new power for the morrow's duties from Thee, Who givest to Thy beloved sleep, though Jesus Christ our Lord. Amen.

Acts of Devotion
From Our Navy Magazine

O Merciful God!

O Merciful God! Eternal Light shining in darkness. Thou Who dispellest the night of sin and all blindness of heart, since Thou hast appointed the night for the rest and the day for labor, we beseech Thee grant that our bodies may rest in peace and quietness, that afterward they may be able to endure the labor they must bear. Temper our sleep that it be not disorderly, that we may remain spotless both in body and soul, yea that even our sleep itself may be to Thy glory. Enlighten the eyes of our understanding that we may not sleep in death but always look for deliverance from this misery. Defend us against all assaults of the devil and take us into Thy holy protection. And although we have not passed this day without greatly sinning against Thee, we beseech Thee to hide our sins with Thy mercy as Thou hidest all things on earth with the darkness of the night, that we may not be cast out from Thy presence. Relieve and comfort all those who are afflicted in mind, body, or estate. Through Jesus Christ, our Lord. Amen.

John Calvin
Soldiers' and Sailors' Prayer Book 1944

A Prayer for the Suffering

Father of mercies and God of all comfort, who in all our affliction art afflicted; look in pity upon all who are suffering in this time of warfare. Protect the defenseless, succour the wounded, receive the dying, and console the anxious and bereaved. Turn the hearts of our enemies, we beseech thee, and forgive both them and us for our share in the sin that has brought this anguish on mankind; open up to us a way of reconciliation and lead us into the path of peace; through Jesus Christ our only Redeemer. Amen.

Divine Service

Prayer by Lieutenant General G. S. Patton, Jr.

God of our Fathers, who by land and sea has ever led us on to victory, please continue Your inspiring guidance in this the greatest of our conflicts.

Strengthen my soul so that the weakening instinct of self-preservation, which besets all of us in battle, shall not blind me to my duty to my own manhood, to the glory of my calling, and to my responsibility to my fellow soldiers.

Grant to our armed forces the disciplined valor and mutual confidence which insures success in war.
Let me not mourn for the men who have died fighting, but rather let me be glad that such heroes have lived.

If it be my lot to die, let me do so with courage and honor in a manner which will bring the greatest harm to the enemy, and please, O Lord, protect and guide those I shall leave behind.

Give us the victory, Lord. Amen.

Lieutenant General G. S. Patton, Jr.
United States Army
Commanding General, Seventh Army

118

From the Retiring Commandant of the United States Marine Corps

O Almighty God, the supreme Governor of all things, whose power no creature is able to resist, to whom it belongeth justly to punish sinners, and to be merciful to those who truly repent: Save and deliver us, we humbly beseech thee, from the hands of our enemies; that we, being armed with thy defense, may be preserved evermore from all perils, to glorify thee, who art the only giver of all victory; through the merits of Thy Son, Jesus Christ our Lord. Amen.

Contributed to this volume as his favorite prayer by
General Thomas Holcomb
Commandant, United States Marine Corps, 1936-1943

Soldiers' and Sailors' Prayer Book 1944

America
Samuel Francis Smith (1831)

My country, 'tis of thee,
Sweet land of liberty,
Of thee I sing;
Land where my fathers died,
Land of the pilgrims' pride,
From ev'ry mountainside
Let freedom ring!.

Our fathers' God to Thee,
Author of liberty,
To Thee we sing.
Long may our land be bright,
With freedom's holy light,
Protect us by Thy might,
Great God our King.

1948

For All in the Service of Our Country

O Almighty Lord God, who neither slumberest nor sleepest; Protect and assist, we beseech thee, all those who at home or abroad, by land, by sea, or in the air, are serving this country, that they, being armed with thy defense, may be preserved evermore in all perils; and being filled with wisdom and girded with strength, may do their duty to thy honour and glory; through Jesus Christ our Lord. Amen.

A Prayer for an Officer Commanding Troops

Father, I pray for these men whom Thou hast entrusted to my leadership. Make me ever remember that each of them is infinitely valuable in Thy sight. I do not pray that Thou wilt perform any miraculous deeds or works of magic to spare their physical lives or my own. I do pray that each of us may do his duty as Thy Son did His and that Thou wilt keep us in Thy care as Thou didst keep Him. Make us faithful unto physical death that we too may find such death the gateway to larger life. Amen.

For the Dying

Unto God's gracious mercy and protection we commit you. The Lord bless you and keep you. The Lord make his face to shine upon you, and be gracious unto you. The Lord lift up his countenance upon you, and give you peace, both now and evermore. Amen.

For Grace to Forgive

Merciful God, in whose dear Son we have redemption, even the forgiveness of sins; Give us such strong belief in this the only power that can abolish evil that we shall be enabled to forgive our enemies; and grant us grace not only to forgive but to accept forgiveness through Christ, the crucified. Amen.

For Control of Speech

O God, who knowest how often we sin against thee with our tongues; Keep us free from all untrue and unkind words; consecrate our speech to thy service; and keep us often silent, that our hearts may speak to thee and may listen for thy voice; through Jesus Christ our Lord. Amen.

For World Peace

Almighty God, from whom all thoughts of truth and peace proceed; Kindle, we pray thee, in the hearts of all men the true love of peace, and guide with thy strong and peaceful wisdom those who take counsel for the nations of the earth, that in tranquility thy kingdom may go forward, till the earth shall be filled with the knowledge of thy love; through Jesus Christ our Lord. Amen.

Eternal God, in whose perfect kingdom no sword is drawn but the sword of righteousness, and no strength known but the strength of love; So guide and inspire, we pray thee, the work of all who seek thy kingdom, that the nations may find their security not in force of arms but in that perfect love which casteth out fear, and in that fellowship revealed to us by thy Son, Jesus Christ our Lord. Amen.

For Justice and Freedom

O God, the King of righteousness, lead us, we pray thee, in ways of justice and peace; inspire us to break down all tyranny and oppression, to gain for every man his due reward, and from every man his due service; that each may live for all and all may care for each, in Jesus Christ our Lord. Amen.

The West Point Cadet Prayer

O God, our father, Thou Searcher of men's hearts, help us to draw near to Thee in sincerity and truth. May our religion be filled with gladness and may our worship of Thee be natural.

Strengthen and increase our admiration for honest dealing and clean thinking, and suffer not our hatred of hypocrisy and pretense ever to diminish. Encourage us in our endeavor to live about the common level of life. Make us to choose the harder right instead of the easier wrong, and never to be content with a half truth when the whole can be won. Endow us with courage that is born of loyalty to all that is noble and worthy, that scorns compromise with vice and injustice and knows no fear when truth and right are in jeopardy. Guard us against flippancy and irreverence in the sacred things of life. Grant us new ties of friendship and new opportunities of service. Kindle our hearts in fellowship with those of a cheerful countenance, and soften our hearts with sympathy for those who sorrow and suffer. Help us, to maintain the honor of the Corps untarnished and unsullied and to show forth in our lives the ideals of West Point in doing our duty to Thee and to our Country. All of which we ask in the name of the Great Friend and Master of men. Amen.

A West Point Prayer

O God, our Father, grant that I may see my Duty not as something forced upon me from outside of myself, but as a sacred privilege with which I have been entrusted; help me to realize that my Honor is my holiest and most priceless possession; and help me to appreciate what a treasured heritage I have in my Country, that so the motto of West Point may become not mere words written for the sight of men's eyes, but a moving force in my life and in that of every man in the Corps. Amen.

A Prayer for the President

O Lord our Governor, whose glory is in all the world; We commend this nation to thy merciful care, that being guided by thy Providence, we may dwell secure in thy peace. Grant to THE PRESIDENT OF THE UNITED STATES, and to all in authority, wisdom and strength to know and to do thy will. Fill them with the love of truth and righteousness, and make them ever mindful of their calling to serve this people in thy fear; through Jesus Christ our Lord, who liveth and reigneth with thee and the Holy Ghost, one God, world without end. Amen.

For Those at Home

Into thy hands, O Father, we commend this day (this night) our homes, families, and all who are dear to us. Bless them with the knowledge of thy continual presence, uphold them in all cares and trials, sustain them with thy power; and grant that, drawing nearer to thee and to each other, we may ever rejoice in the fellowship of those who trust in thy goodness and thy love; through Jesus Christ our Lord. Amen.

For Those We Love

O Thou who hast ordered this wondrous world, who knowest all things in earth and heaven; so fill our hearts with trust in thee, that by night and by day, at all times and in all seasons, we may without fear commit those who are dear to us to thy never-failing love, for this life and the life to come. Amen.

For Prisoners

We Beseech thee, O God, for all prisoners and captives, and all who suffer from oppression, that thou wilt manifest thy mercy toward them, and make the heart of man merciful as thine own; through Jesus Christ our Lord. Amen.

For One Departed

Almighty God, we remember this day before thee thy faithful servant (N.), and we pray thee that, having opened to him the gates of larger life, thou wilt receive him more and more into thy joyful service; that he may win, with thee and thy servants everywhere, the eternal victory; through Jesus Christ our Lord. Amen.

For a Recovery from Sickness

O God, who art the giver of life, of health, and of safety; We bless thy Name, that thou hast been pleased to deliver from his bodily sickness this thy servant, who now desireth to return thanks unto thee, in the presence of all thy people. Gracious art thou, O Lord, and full of compassion to the children of men. May his heart be duly impressed with a sense of thy merciful goodness, and may he devote the residue of his days to an humble, holy, and obedient walking before thee; through Jesus Christ our Lord. Amen.

For Those Who Mourn

Almighty God, Father of mercies and giver of all comfort; Deal graciously, we pray thee, with all those who mourn, that, casting every care on thee, they may know the consolation of thy love; through Jesus Christ our Lord. Amen.

For Those Wounded in War

O Lord, we pray thee to have mercy upon all who are this day wounded and suffering. Though kindred and friends be far away, let thy grace be their comfort. Raise them to health again, if it be thy good pleasure; but chiefly give them patience and faith in thee; through Jesus Christ our Lord. Amen.

In Time of War

O God, who seest that in this warfare we are seeking to serve thee, and yet in the waging of it must needs do many things that are an offence against thy love; Accept we pray thee, our imperfect offering. Arm us with thy Spirit that our warfare may further the victory of thy justice and truth; through Jesus Christ our Lord. Amen.

For the Army

O Lord God of Hosts, stretch forth, we pray thee, thine almighty arm to strengthen and protect the soldiers of our country. Support them in the day of battle and in the time of peace keep them safe from all evil; endue them with courage and loyalty; and grant that in all things they may serve without reproach; through Jesus Christ our Lord. Amen.

For Our Country

Almighty God, who hast given us this good land for our heritage;
We humbly beseech thee that we may always prove ourselves a
people mindful of thy favor and glad to do thy will. Bless our land
with honorable industry, sound learning, and pure manners. Save
us from violence, discord and confusion; from pride and arrogance,
and from every evil way. Defend our liberties, and fashion into one
united people the multitudes brought hither out of many kindreds
and tongues. Endue with the spirit of wisdom those to whom in thy
Name we entrust the authority of government, that there may be
justice and peace at home, and that, through obedience to thy law,
we may show forth thy praise among the nations of the earth. In
the time of prosperity, fill our hearts with thankfulness, and in the
day of trouble, suffer not our trust in thee to fail; all which we ask
through Jesus Christ our Lord. Amen.

The West Point Prayer Book 1948

To God Be the Glory
Fanny J. Crosby (1875)

To God be the glory, great things He has done;
So loved He the world that He gave us His Son,
Who yielded His life an atonement for sin,
And opened the life gate that all may go in.

Refrain:
Praise the Lord, praise the Lord,
Let the earth hear His voice!
Praise the Lord, praise the Lord,
Let the people rejoice!
O come to the Father, through Jesus the Son,
And give Him the glory, great things He has
done.

1951

Memorial Prayer

O God, by whose grace thy people gain courage in the way of the heroes of faith, we lift our hearts in gratitude for all who have lived valiantly, and for all who have died bravely for truth, and liberty, and righteousness. Especially do we thank Thee for the heroes of the common good, who suffered and made trial of bitter sacrifice in achieving the freedom of religious worship and the measure of social and political and economic liberty we enjoy in this good land. God of our Fathers, help us to prize very highly, and to guard very carefully the gifts which their loyalty and devotion have passed on to us. Grant unto us the gift of a living and vigorous faith, that we may be like the heroes: that we may be true as they were true, that we may be loyal as they were loyal, and that we may serve our country and the cause of pure religion all the days of our lives; and grant that we with all those who depart hence in the faith of thy holy name, may wear at last the victor's crown. Through Jesus Christ our Lord. Amen.

From the Commander in Chief of the United States Fleet

For Christmas

Almighty God, who by the birth of thy Son hast given us a great light to draw upon our darkness: Grant, we pray thee, that in his light we may see light. Let the light of Christ search our souls and scatter our darkness. Let it shine more and more throughout the world unto the perfect day; and give us grace while we have the light to walk in the light, that we may be the children of light. Amen.

For Lent

Almighty and everlasting God, who hatest nothing that thou hast made, and dost forgive the sins of all those who are penitent: Create and make in us new and contrite hearts, that we, being truly sorry for our sins and acknowledging our faults, may obtain of thee, God of all mercy, perfect remission and forgiveness; through Jesus Christ our Lord. Amen.

Palm Sunday

Almighty and everlasting God, who, of thy tender love towards mankind, hast sent thy Son, our Saviour Jesus Christ, to take upon him our flesh, and to suffer death upon the cross, that all mankind should follow the example of his great humility: Mercifully grant that we may both follow the example of his patience, and also be made partakers of his resurrection; through the same Jesus Christ our Lord. Amen.

Good Friday

O Merciful God, who hast made all men, and hatest nothing that thou hast made, nor desirest the death of a sinner, but rather that he should be converted and live: Have mercy upon all who know thee not, as thou art revealed in the gospel of thy Son. Take from them all ignorance, hardness of heart, and contempt of thy Word; and so fetch them home, blessed Lord, to thy fold; that they may be made one flock under one shepherd, Jesus Christ our Lord, who liveth and reigneth with thee and the Holy Spirit, and God, world without end. Amen.

Easter

Almighty God, who hast brought again from the dead our Lord
Jesus, the Prince of Life, giving him victory over death and the
grave: Grant us power, we beseech thee, to rise with him to newness
of life; that we may overcome the world with the victory of faith,
and share in the eternal joy of the just; through the grace of the just;
though the grace of that risen Saviour, who liveth and reigneth with
thee, world without end. Amen.

Prayer for Our Country

Almighty God, Who has given us this god land for our heritage, we
humbly beseech Thee that we may always prove ourselves a people
mindful of thy favor and glad to do thy will. Bless our land with
honorable industry, sound learning, and pure manners. Save us
from violence, discord, and confusion; from pride and arrogancy
and from every evil way. Defend our liberties and fashion into one
united people the multitudes brought hither out of many kindreds
and tongues. Endue with the spirit of wisdom those to whom in thy
Name we entrust the authority of government, that there may be
justice and peace at home and that through obedience to thy law we
may show forth thy praise among the nations of the earth. In the
time of prosperity fill our hearts with thankfulness, and in the day
of trouble suffer not our trust in Thee to fail. Through Jesus Christ
our Lord. Amen.

A Prayer of Cleansing

Almighty God, unto whom all hearts are open, all desires known,
and from whom no secrets are hid: Cleanse the thoughts of our
hearts by the inspiration of thy Holy Spirit, that we may perfectly
love thee, and worthily magnify thy holy name; through Christ our
Lord. Amen.

A Prayer of Protection for Airmen

Our Heavenly Father, whose loving care encompasses even the sparrow in its flight, guide and protect, we pray, the men who fly the uncharted spaces of the sky. Bless those who, through service in the Air Force, stand guard over the sacred trust of home and country.

Endow them with wisdom and understanding that they may clearly see the path of duty and courageously devote themselves in service to the nation they love. In the solitude of flight may the beauty of Thy greatness be revealed to each of them that they may pattern their lives after Thine.

Armed Forces Hymnal 195X
(Publication date unknown)

Strength, Care and Peace

Extend Thy strengthening presence to those who wait at home; and may they ever know Thy watchful care will keep safe the absent one.

Let Thy benediction be upon us, O God we pray. Lead us to carry on the trust left by our brothers, who gave with honor their lives in service of their country. May we find peace in the knowledge of our missions accomplished and their task completed through service for Thee. Amen.

General Hoyt S. Vandenberg (1899–1954)
Commander of the Air Force

Thy Blessings O Lord

Almighty God:

May those who have given their lives in the service of this nation rest in Thy care.

May those who are wounded in body find spiritual comfort under Thy guidance in the knowledge that through their services a great cause has been served.

May those who offer their lives in support of that cause, by land and sea and air, find strength in Thy divine guidance.

May those of us who serve this nation in its great purpose to secure freedom for all peoples be sustained by Thy blessings.

Give us strength, O Lord, that we may be pure in heart and in purpose to the end that there may be peace on earth and good will among men.

May we be mindful this Easter morning still stands Thine ancient sacrifice, an humble and a contrite heart. Amen.

General George C. Marshall
Chief of Staff of the Army, Secretary of State,
and Secretary of Defense

A Prayer for Safety

Dear Father in Heaven;

We thank Thee for Thy Son, who showed us the way to come to you as Our Father. Tonight and always we ask Thee to be with our boys in each branch of the service. Many are so young, and perhaps have not had the guiding hand of parents and the church. We pray especially for these. That they may come to know and trust Thee.

Keep my own boys free from hatred, except for that which is evil. Never let intolerance for those of different race, color, or creed enter their minds. Fill them with understanding, that they may love their enemies. But give them courage and determination to destroy the wickedness these represent. Hold them in Thy hand, give them Faith and courage in their darkest hours. May they help others to know Thy presence and power. Be with Thy Chaplains, as they comfort and care for the souls of men and women, so precious to Thee.

If it be in Thy Great Plan, bring my boys safely home again. Yet if Thy Will directs them to Eternity, help us to understand and be worthy of their trust, that we may meet them there some day. Keep me humble, Lord. Direct my words and living that I may share the Faith and Peace Thou hast given me. Use our united prayers to overwhelm evil. Our sons are in Thy watch, Thy care, and Thy will.

In the Name of Jesus who gave His Life that we might have Life Everlasting. Amen.

Mrs. C. R. Tilghman
A mother of two sons in the service.

The Serviceman's Prayer (God Be with You)

Heavenly Father, I commit myself body and soul to Thy keeping. When I am in peril of life give me courage to do my duty. When I am tempted to sin give me strength to resist. If I am sick or wounded grant me healing. If I fall, or Thy mercy receive me to thyself, forgive me all my sins. Bless all who are near and dear to me and keep them in Thy fatherly care. And in Thy good providence, out of this evil bring a lasting peace; through Jesus Christ our Lord. Amen.

Bishop Henry Wise Hobson (1891-1983)

Courage and Persistence

Father of all mercies, and Father of Thine only begotten Son, who is our Lord and Saviour, I come seeking courage and persistence to complete my training, that I may be a good soldier of my country. May I get ready here to make my life count for freedom and an enduring peace. In my loneliness may I have Thy presence, and with Thy Grace may I conquer homesickness and doubt.

May I be faithful. May I have the assurance that all is well with my loved ones, that they too are in Thy care, and that in our separation we shall find in our memories comfort and power. As a son I pray to Thee in the name of Thine own Son, Jesus Christ our Lord. Amen.

Daniel A. Poling

Grant Me Courage

God grant me the courage to change the things I can change, the serenity to accept those I cannot change, and the wisdom to know the difference -- but God grant me the courage not to give up on what I think is right even though I think it is hopeless. Amen.

Five-Star Admiral Chester W. Nimitz (1885-1966)
Commander in Chief, United States Pacific Fleet

Gird Us With Thy Strength

God, our Father, infinite in understanding and mighty in battle, be with us, your soldiers, wherever we serve. Keep us ever conscious of Thee and with Thy strength sustain us. While peace endures give us energy in the good cause; help us to cultivate our skills and instill in us the personal devotion to duty that questions not and knows no reservation. Help us to realize our responsibilities as Americans. Keep us ever conscious of our Country's ideals and suffer us never to tarnish our soldier's honor.

When war comes, O Lord, gird us with Thy strength, and give to us the comforting knowledge of Thy imminence in the awful loneliness of battle. Grant us the strength of righteousness, not of ourselves but of our cause. Purge us of personal pride and conceit. Help us to lead with justice and human understanding those entrusted to our command; and to fulfill the purposes of our superiors with cheerful vigor and effectiveness. Help us to carry our lives but lightly when weighed in the balance against the ultimate values for which our Nation fights. Grant us steadfastness under fire, courage in adversity, fortitude in pain. Bless and sustain our fellow soldiers and grant us long and joyful strength of their comradeship. Ease the wounded and stricken, O Lord. Comfort, guide, and keep us; and teach us how with faith to endure hardness as good soldiers of Jesus Christ, and of our Country. Amen.

Maj. General Bryant E. Moore
Commander of the 8th Infantry Division during and after WWII

Lift Up Our Eyes

O, Lord, unto Thee we lift up our eyes in our hour of trouble as we know Thou art with us and watching over us. Yea, though we walk through the Valley of the Shadow of Death, we will fear no evil, for Thou art with us, Thy rod and Thy staff they comfort us.

A thousand shall fall at our side and ten thousand at our right hand, but with Thy protection, we feel it will not come nigh us.

May our sin of worry be forgiven, O Father, for we have doubted Thy power and Thy goodness too often. Shake our souls this day with Thy power, and as we contemplate the awesome magnitude of the world to be, let our spirits grow in statue and in power. Help us to live as Thy sons, as free men, as heirs of Christ and thus prepare the way for the gathering of all nations into Thy family until Peace shall reign forever, and all peoples shall proclaim Thee Lord of Lords and King of Kings. Amen.

Captain Eddie Rickenbacker (1890-1973)
WWI Fighter Ace and Medal of Honor Recipient

A Prayer for Courage to Face Risk

O God, who knowest the duties that be ahead of us, and the weaknesses that easily beset us, prepare us for the unknown immediately before us. We do not pray for immunity from risks; we pray for courage to face risks. We do not ask to be spared from danger; we ask for strength to face danger resolutely. Grant that we may be able to finish that which Thou hast granted us the wish to begin; through Jesus Christ, our Lord. Amen.

General Mark W. Clark (1896-1984)
Allied Commander in Italy during WWI

A Prayer for Sustaining Power

Our Father, Lord of earth and seas,

We who are forced into conflict to uphold those principles in which we believe --

We who are also dedicated to saving lives from peril, in war and peace--

Ask Thy help.
>   Give us courage in danger,
>   Endurance in exhausting toil and stress,
>   Grant us inner calmness of spirit in stormy seas and in heat of battle,
>   So that we may uphold our country's ideals and our honor,
>   To Thy greater glory and to the peace of mankind,
>   In Jesus' name. Amen

Commander Russell Waesche (1886-1946)
Eighth Commandant of the United States Coast Guard

Prayer for Victory Over Thy Adversary

Have mercy on us, O God of the universe, and behold us, and send Thy fear upon all the nations.

Lift up Thy hand against the strange nations, that they may see Thy power.

As in their sight Thou hast shown Thyself holy in us, so in our sight show Thyself glorious in them, so they may know, even as we know, that there is no God beside Thee, O Lord.

Renew Thy signs and repeat Thy wonders; glorify Thy hand and Thy right arm.

Stir up anger and pour forth fury; take away the adversary and destroy the enemy.

Hasten the time and fix the end, that they may declare Thy great works.

Fill Zion with Thy praises, and Thy temple with Thy glory.
Amen.

Brig. General James H. O'Neill
Deputy Chief of Chaplains, served with General Patton in WWII

Watch Over Us

Dear Lord,

I turn to Thee as my partner and comrade. Stay close by and help me to be always near to Thee. With complete trust I put my loved ones and myself in Thy hands. I know Thou wilt watch over them and me. Help me, dear Lord, to live, and if it be Thy will, to die as a Christian clean of soul and with love in my heart. Help me at all times to keep the faith. In Christ's name I pray. Amen.

Dr. Norman Vincent Peale (1898-1993)
Minister and Author, most notably of *The Power of Positive Thinking*

A Prayer for Practical Faith

Our Heavenly Father, I need faith for here and now. Faith for the little things that make up my day. Faith to carry me through the drudgery and unpleasantness of camp life. Faith to meet temptations--temptations to shirk, to alibi, to take advantage, to doubt my comrades and myself.

O God, in Thine infinite knowledge and with power to create worlds, create in me courage just for this day. Give to me now a sense of being needed. Make my country real to me and her cause so ample that in everything I am called upon to do, however small the task, I shall feel that I am indispensable!

Father, may I have here and now the assurance that Thou dost hear and answer me. Through Jesus Christ our Lord. Amen

Daniel A. Poling

Teach Us Thy Truth

General Clay writes: "Perhaps I should not say so but my prayers are usually silent prayers, and I find difficulty in expressing them in specific words. If I could express the prayer which is most often in my heart, it would be":

Our Father Who art in Heaven, open up the hearts and minds of men to Thy truth. Teach us that power comes from helping our fellow man and not from destroying him to satisfy ruthless personal ambition. Give us the strength to be patient and yet to be determined. Bear with us and bless us now in our hour of trial so that with steadfast purpose we may pursue the cause of freedom until there is peace and understanding among men everywhere. Amen.

General Lucius D. Clay (1897-1978)
Deputy to General Dwight D. Eisenhower

Justice Among the Nations

Almighty God, who hast created man in Thine own image; grant us grace fearlessly to contend against evil, and to make no peace with oppression; and, that we may reverently use our freedom, help us to employ it in the maintenance of justice among men and nations, to the glory of Thy holy Name; through Jesus Christ, our Lord. Amen.

Dean Acheson (1893-1971)
Secretary of State

Deliverance from Oppressors

Accompanying the prayer of General Klein, is this message: "I wish to express the deep-seated conviction that this book of prayers will be warmly received by a world which is very much in need of closer contact with God."

Our Father. Whose glory filleth the Universe, we reflect upon the great achievements of those who have made the extreme sacrifice for our country in order that our blessed land may continue to be a beacon of light and a source of hope for the entire civilized world.

Deliver us, O Heavenly Father, from our present impending evils and frustrate the designs of our enemies. Restore us to the bosom of peace.

We pray to Thee to hasten the day when humanity shall be delivered from oppressors and oppression and hate and violence shall never again flourish on the face of Thy earth, and may we realize in our day the fulfillment of the prophetic vision "that they shall dwell every man under his own vine and fig tree with none to make them afraid." Amen.

Brig. General Julius Klein (1894-1976)

Be With Me God

Dear God, compassionate Father, be with me now and always.
Guide me through this night and the day beyond. Strengthen me
to endure, enable me to accomplish, speak to me above the noise
of terror and destruction, grant me the courage to meet whatever
comes. And bless, dear Lord, my comrades; sustain and keep in
safety all those I love, in Jesus' Name. Amen.

Faith Baldwin (1893-1978)

*In sending her prayer, Faith Baldwin writes of her nephew, Bruce, who was
killed in action in Korea: "He volunteered...they were ambushed...he and a
few of his men escaped and got in the clear....Other men were trapped, and
with the captain of another unit they fought back with one tank and rescued
many...Bruce was killed." He was as her own son.*

Blessings and Guidance

Christ has said, "if ye forgive men their trespasses, your heavenly
Father will forgive you. And whatsoever ye shall ask in my name,
that will I do, that the Father may be glorified in the Son." In Thy
name, dear Jesus, we ask Thy blessing and guidance in our daily
tasks, in order that Thy will may be done and all peoples be made to
know Thy desires. Amen.

Charles W. Skeele
President of the Reserve Officers Association

Guide Us, Father

Our Heavenly Father,

In these days of anxiety and confusion we look to Thee for guidance we so greatly need. Take under Thy direction the talents and abilities that are ours and indicate to us the manner in which these abilities may be used for Thee.

If today we are called upon to meet the challenge of life and our reservoir of personal strength is insufficient, grant us the sustaining power of Thy presence that we may, with Thee, acquit ourselves well.

Into Thy care this day we commit our loved ones. Thou knowest the deep thoughts of our hearts concerning them and the good things we covet for them. Today make it possible for us to enrich their lives through our love. Keep them safe in Thy care.

Grant this day, our Father, Thy blessing upon our nation. The strength and greatness of our nation will be only in proportion to our strong and our greatness. Use us, we pray, to build a better nation and a better world.

Stay near us this day, Father, for without Thee we are indeed weak, but with Thee we can do all things. Amen.

Major General Charles I. Carpenter (1906-1994)
Chief of Air Force Chaplains

I Offer To Thee This Day

My God, I offer to Thee this day
All that I can think, or do, or say;
Uniting it with what was done
On earth by Jesus Christ, Thy son.
Amen.

General Clifton B. Cates (1893-1970)
The Commandant of the Marine Corps

A Prayer for Daily Help

O God, our Heavenly Father,

We rejoice in the fact that Thou knowest the way we take; that Thou knowest all our needs; and that Thou knowest where we are strong and where we are weak. Help us to find the companionship of Thy presence. Make us strong through the grace which Thou dost offer and lead us into the way of truth and peace through Thy spirit.

We pray Thee, help us daily to live fully committed to those high purposes which moved Thee to give Thy Son Jesus Christ as our Saviour and Lord. We pray for Thy light and Thy salvation. Forgive our sins. Take from our lives the strain and stress. Renew a right spirit within us and help us to respond to Thy love and grace so freely offered. In our conduct may we daily express thy order. In our lives may Thy concern for human welfare find a hearty response. In all of our experiences help us to know that Thy love is overshadowing us and Thy arms are upholding us. We thank Thee also for Thy grace, through which we are saved. May the light of Thy countenance shine upon our path, and may we walk in that light. Bless all who are associated with us in this service to our nation and for humanity. We pray for Thy Spirit to lead all those who direct in the ordering of human relations and establishment of world peace. Hasten the day when there shall be peace and righteousness for all men everywhere.

This we pray in the name of him who is the Prince of Peace, Jesus Christ our Lord. Amen

Bishop John S. Stamm (1878-1956)
President of the Federal Council of Churches of Christ in America

A Prayer When Far From Home

Dear Lord, I am far from my loved ones but not alone;
Miles away from my friends but I have a Friend.
My heart is filled with courage and I have hope,
For Thou art with me.
Thou art the light that fills my soul with brightness and with joy.
I shall lean upon Thee and not fall.
I shall accomplish the task I have set out to do and not fail;
With Thy help nobody can fail.
I love thee, O Lord, my God, with all my heart,
with all my soul and with all my might,
And I know Thou dost love me and will care for me.
Amen.

Dr. Edgar Magnin (1890-1984)
Rabbi of the Wilshire Boulevard Temple

For Spiritual Renewal

Eternal Spirit, Who art the Source of all excellence, inspire us today
as though the sun of a new spiritual springtime had risen upon us.
Carry us out of inner darkness and gloom into light, out of our
deadness of heart into life, out of our barrenness into fruitfulness
and the promise of a good harvest.

We need Thee in our troubles, for they are many. We must choose
between faith and fear, courage and cynicism, strength of character
and collapse of life; and we would choose the better way. Therefore
we seek in Thee vision and power and hope. Grant us grace to
accept and to use them worthily. Open our eyes to see opportunity
here where we stand, and to see resources of strength here where
we struggle.

Come close to us one by one in strong temptation, in moral defeat,
in perplexity; and grant unto us some visitation of the Divine that
will lift us up, increase our courage, strengthen our faith, bring us to
victory. We ask it in the Spirit of Christ. Amen.

Pastor Harry Emerson Fosdick (1878-1969)

Commit Without Fear

O Thou Who has ordered this wondrous world, Who knowest all things in earth and heaven, so fill our hearts with trust in Thee, that by night and by day, at all times and in all seasons, we may without fear commit those who are dear to us to Thy never-failing love, for this life and the life to come; through Jesus Christ our Lord. Amen.

Mrs. Grace Coolidge (1879-1957)
Wife of the President of the United States

Fill Us With Thy Love

Dear Father:

Through the guidance of the Holy Spirit help us to face this day with the confidence of Thy Presence in our hearts, so that we may be a blessing to someone, be a comfort to someone.

Fill us with Thy Love.

The Love that passeth all understanding.

We long for the Beauty of Jesus to shine through all that we do each moment of today.

And help us to live that we may look forward with joyful anticipation to our certain reunion with the ones we love who are just a little ahead of us. They are already in Thy presence. And we love them now even as we loved them when they walked beside us.

Amen.

Mrs. Gipsy Smith
Widow of a famous evangelist who was a Chaplain in WWI

For the Leadership of America

Almighty and everlasting God, from Whom every good and perfect gift proceeds, look down upon us, Thy children, whom Thou hast made to Thine own image and likeness.

Uphold the hands of those who make the laws by which we are governed: uphold the hands of those who enforce those laws. Enlighten our intellects, inflame our hearts and strengthen our wills to persevere in the path of truth and righteousness.

We invoke Thy divine blessing upon the President of these United States of America, upon all the officers of our land, legislative, executive, and judicial.

We ask Thy blessing upon all the officers and members of our armed forces and upon all citizens of our beloved country...

Let Thy divine benediction shine upon and gladden the hearts of all officers and members of this glorious organization, The Marine Corps League.

Hasten the time, Almighty God, Our Father, when the spirit of the charity of God shall so prevail throughout the world that no nation shall wage war for the purpose of aggression and none shall need it as a means of defense. Amen.

Theus J. MacQueen
National Commander of the Marine Corps League,
written by M.A. Hally, Marine Corps Chaplain

Riches For All Men

Oh, give us riches, of love's glorious kind, That come from openness of heart and mind! Recall to us the story which doth say

When base or cruel men do pass this way
Nothing at all is freely offered then
Save hollow echoes- yet how wondrous when
A man impelled by guileless love goes by:
The very gold deep in the earth doth cry;
"Take me and use me for the greater good
For all creation and for brotherhood."
Amen.

Mrs. Robert Patterson
Wife for the former Secretary of War, Judge Robert Patterson

Prayer for a Son Overseas

Our Heavenly Father, we bring to Thee our Son. In a place distant from us and yet always near to Thee, he serves his country and the cause of Brotherhood and Peace. Our love follows him, but our arms are too short to reach him there. In our weakness we come to Thy strength. Wilt Thou make him strong and keep him clean and fit?

We ask for our son not favors we would not seek for all sons, but he is of our blood, and to us a sacred trust from Thee. Make our faith strong that we fail him not.

We do not ask that he be delivered from hardships or made exempt from burdens and suffering that in the line of duty he must bear. We do pray that he have courage, and that he be made adequate. Our hearts hunger for him, and in Thy Will we pray for his return. Make us worthy of the answer to our prayer. Through Jesus Christ our Lord. Amen.

Daniel A. Poling

Prayer of a Soldier

Our Heavenly Father, grant peace of mind to those whom I have left behind me. May they be comforted by their memories of all they did and gave to make me ready for life. May they know, as I can never tell them, how grateful I am for their loyalty, their love, and their sacrifices. May my letters to them and all the words unspoken that I would write sustain and strengthen them, and may they somehow know how real is their help to me now, how clearly I feel them with me in this place, and how their faith in me makes and keeps me strong.

Our Father, I thank Thee for them. Make and keep me worthy of them. Through Jesus Christ our Lord. Amen

Daniel A. Poling

The Prayer of a Midshipman

Almighty Father, whose way is in the sea, whose paths are in the great waters, whose command is over all and whose love never faileth: Let me be aware of Thy presence and obedient to Thy will. Keep me true to my best self, guarding me against dishonesty in purpose and in deed, and helping me so to live that I can stand unashamed and unafraid before my shipmates, my loved ones, and Thee. Protect those in whose love I live. Give me the will to do the work of a man and to accept my share of responsibilities with a strong heart and a cheerful mind. Make me faithful to my duties and mindful of the traditions of the Service of which I am a part. If I am inclined to doubt, steady my faith; if I am tempted, make me strong to resist; if I should miss the mark, give me courage to try again. Guide me with the light of truth and keep before me the life of Him by Whose example and help I trust to obtain the answer to my prayer, Jesus Christ, our Lord. Amen.

Vice-Admiral Harry W. Hill (1890-1971)
Superintendent, United States Naval Academy
Favorite prayer of Admiral Forrest Sherman,
Chief of Naval Operations

A Sailor's Prayer

Lord Jesus, Thy almighty hand has made the earth and sky and sea. Thou art the omnipotent Ruler of the mighty waters of the deep. Wherever my duties in the service of my country take me, even though it be to the uttermost parts of the sea, I know that even there Thy hand shall lead me, and Thy right hand shall hold me. Those were the hands that were extended on the cross for my salvation, the hands on which no power of earth and hell shall pluck me. O Jesus, be Thou at all times my mighty Protector, my gracious Guide, my very present Help in all trouble. Preserve and strengthen me in Thy faith, so that I may never cast aside my trust in Thy atoning blood. Keep me in chastity, in loyal and courageous service of my country. Teach me to submit willingly to all tasks assigned to me by my superiors. When dangerous storms arise, hold Thy guarding hand over our ship and its entire crew, and dispel all fear and terror by the knowledge that Thou art mightier than the mightiest waves, and that Thou canst protect Thy children in the raging of wind and billows. May Thy peace keep my whole spirit, that my soul and body be preserved blameless until the great day of Thy coming, my Redeemer and Lord. Amen.

Reverend Roy B. Schmeichel
The National Chaplain, Veterans of Foreign Wars

Army Nurse's Prayer

Father, the soldier seems so close to You,
I wonder if his hours on earth are few;
His manly face is hot and red,
Seems I see angels around his bed.
Help me to keep him safe lest I should fail
My pledge of love to Florence Nightingale.
If he should die then I will know
You called him home 'cause You loved him so;
But, Father, ere he goes to rest
Help me to know I have done my best. Amen.

Col. Mary Philips by Edith Aynes

God's Presence

Our Father Who art in Heaven, Who through Christ our Lord hast taught us that Thou art near us on earth:

We stand today, uncovered, desiring the consciousness of Thy presence, in faith that while we are at one in spirit with the heroes of the common good we are not far from Thee.

Give us to know the power of the lives this day commemorates. Bring vividly before our vision all who have hazarded their lives for country and home, and make real to our hearts the faith and the courage by which our fathers and our comrades lived and died. May our minds be open to every sacred memory, and may our hearts be receptive to every holy impression.

Here in the awareness of Thy presence we would dedicate ourselves anew, in confidence that life's battle is not lost and that our comrades have not died in vain. Consecrate with Thy presence the way our feet must go, and lift us above bitterness, and hate, and unrighteous anger into faith and courage and good will. Guard us against violence of spirit and preserve us in mental and spiritual health, that whatever bodily sacrifice awaits us, we may endure with patience, keeping faith with ourselves, our loved ones, and with Thee.

Comfort the sorrowing, soothe the suffering, and be near to bless the dying, granting them the preparation of the gospel of peace for the life beyond. Remember in mercy the children of Thy creation, and bring us out of our confusion and strife to know that the fruits of righteousness shall be peace. Through Christ our Lord. Amen.

Colonel Ivan L. Bennett
General MacArthur's Senior Chaplain

Prayer of Discernment

Our Father God, who hath made and preserved us a nation: Our fathers trusted in Thee and were not confounded. In Thee we trust.

Thou hast taught us to love truth and beauty and goodness. In all our relationships as citizens of the Republic, this sweet land of liberty, may Thy truth make us free--free from littleness, pride, and prejudice, and from all the ugly sins of disposition which so easily do beset us. May our patriotism be pure and undefiled. In all our aspirations and attitudes lift us, we pray Thee, above the mud and scum of mere things to the holiness of Thy beauty. Thus may the common tasks and the trivial rounds be edged with crimson and gold.

Lead us in the paths of righteousness for Thy Name's sake. Enrich us with those durable satisfactions of life, so that the multiplying years may not find us bankrupt in those things that matter most, the golden currency of faith and hope and love.

In these desperate and dangerous days in our national life, when the precious things we hold nearest our hearts are threatened by the sinister forces without pity or conscience, help us to give the best that is in us against the wrong that needs resistance, and for the right that needs assistance and for the future in the distance, and the good that we may do.

In this solemn hour of the supreme test of America's faith, may we bear our full part in freedom's daughters who will live in the light of the new day: "I saw the powers of darkness put to flight. I saw the morning break!"

We ask it in the dear Redeemer's name. Amen.

Dr. Frederick Brown Harris (1883-1970)
Chaplain of the United States Senate

A Prayer for Our Country

Almighty God, our Heavenly Father, we praise Thee for our homeland which we lovingly call America. We remember with thankful hearts the courage and sacrifice that went into the building of our country. We cherish the memory of the heroic men and women who made possible its growth and progress. We think of its rich resources of mine and mountain, river and forest, soil and climate. Beyond everything else, we are grateful for the Christian tradition out of which everything has come. May we increasingly feel that a nation is great only as it walks in the paths of righteousness. Help us so to live and act that we may be worthy trustees of the moral heritage of America. Amen.

Dr. Harry N. Holmes (1879-1958)
Honorary Secretary of the
World's Christian Endeavor Union

Prayer for Our Children

Guide our steps, O Lord, that they may grow in wisdom and understanding of Thy ways. Give them the zeal to work and teach them the joy that comes from tasks well done. Fill their hearts with love and compassion for their fellow men; in meekness and humility let them serve. With the courage to stand for right and justice and peace, may they play fair in the game of life, and grant them vision and purpose. Teach them to believe first in Thee, and believing in Thee, to believe in themselves. This, O Lord, I ask for our children. Amen.

Ethel B. Sager
Former Dean of Ottawa Hills High School for Girls
and Special Lecturer at Toledo University

Remembering Comrades

O God, we pray Thee that the memory of our comrades, fallen in battle, may be ever sound in our hearts; that the sacrifice which they have offered for our country's cause may be acceptable in Thy sight; and that an entrance into Thine eternal peace may, by Thy pardoning grace, be open unto them through Jesus Christ our Lord and Saviour. Amen.

A Prayer for Protection

Our gracious Heavenly Father, we commend to Thy loving care all those who have gone forth to serve their country and the cause of freedom, on land and sea and in the air. Keep them strong and steadfast; give them courage and chivalry; shield them from danger; inspire them with devotion to the cause for which they are offering their lives, and help them and us to achieve a just and lasting peace for the world.

Have mercy, O Lord, upon all the wounded and suffering. Though kindred and friends be far away, may Thy grace be their comfort. Uphold by Thy strength and guide by Thy holy spirit all those who care for the sick and wounded this day.

We would remember before Thee in our prayer, all little children and their mothers - those who are lonely, forlorn, and made homeless by war. Help us to be helpers of the helpless in this world of fear and strife.

God bless America. We pray that Thou wilt keep our nation in Thy holy protection for the bringing in of the glad day of peace with justice. Speed the day, O Lord, when all men shall brothers be and when the kingdoms of this world shall become the Kingdoms of our God and His Christ. We pray in His name, Amen.

Dr. Jesse M. Bader (1886-1963)
Executive Secretary of the Department of Evangelism of the
Federal Council of the Churches of Christ in America

In Gratitude

Eternal God, our Heavenly Father, from the midst of the manifold blessings Thou hast sent our way, we lift our hearts to Thee in gratitude.

We thank Thee for our Nation. We love it and are striving to make it a righteous ministering nation. We love our flag and pray Thee to help us to keep it unstained and victorious. In the days of prosperity fill our hearts with thankfulness, and in the time of sorrow suffer not our trust in Thee to fail. Deepen by Thy spirit our devotion to Thee and Thy Church. Help us to stand fast against everything that would defeat the cause of peace and brotherhood. Endow with wisdom those to whom we have entrusted the authority to govern and direct the destinies of our nation.

Help us to make clear choice of the road we are to follow and give us a faith daring enough to press on toward the Kingdom of God, even if the way is not always clear. Keep us clean in life, steady in purpose, and bring us at last through Thy mercy to the inheritance of those who endure. In the name of the Saviour of the world, the Lord Jesus Christ, we pray. Amen.

Bishop Arthur J. Moore
The Armed Forces Prayer Book 1951

For the Coast Guard

O Lord, who of old didst still the raging of the sea, watch over, we beseech thee, the men of the Coast Guard as they sail upon their missions of helpfulness and succour. Grant them courage and skill and a safe return, and a grateful sense of thy mercy toward them; through the same Jesus Christ our Lord. Amen.

For The Air Force

O Lord God of hosts, who stretchest out the heavens like a curtain; Watch over and protect, we pray thee, the airmen of our country as they fly upon their appointed tasks. Give them courage as they face the foe, and skill in the performance of their duty. Sustain them with thy Everlasting Arms. May thy hand lead them and thy right hand hold them up that they may return to the earth with a grateful sense of thy mercy; through Jesus Christ our Lord. Amen.

For Our Enemies

O Saviour of the world, our Redeemer, whose love embraces all mankind, we hear thy prayer from the Cross: "Father, forgive them, for they know not what they do." Forgive, O Lord, those who have poured out the innocent blood and caused suffering in the world. May our prayers be for them a ministry of reconciliation. We ask it in thine own Name. Amen.

The Armed Forces Prayer Book 1951,
The Protestant Episcopal Church

A Mighty Fortress is Our God
Martin Luther (1529)

A mighty fortress is our God, a bulwark never failing;
Our helper He, amid the flood of mortal ills prevailing:
For still our ancient foe doth seek to work us woe;
His craft and power are great, and, armed with cruel hate,
On earth is not his equal.

Did we in our own strength confide, our striving would be losing;
Were not the right Man on our side, the Man of God's own choosing:
Dost ask who that may be? Christ Jesus, it is He;
Lord Sabaoth, His Name, from age to age the same,
And He must win the battle.

1966

Prayer For Atonement

My Jesus, crucified for love of us, scourged and crowned with thorns by our sins, I ardently desire, to the utmost of my powers, to make atonement for all my own sins and those of all Your creatures. I am deeply sorry for all the faults and sins whereby I have offended You, from the first instant of my awakening intelligence, and for all other sins from the beginning of the world. I detest and regret them because they have offended You, who are so good and worthy of my love. I ardently desire and purpose to redouble my efforts to serve and please You hereafter, in atonement and reparation for all sins. I intend in all things to seek Your glory, to do Your will, to accomplish perfectly all that You desire. I yearn and wish that all other creatures may likewise serve and please You perfectly, for Your pure love.

In atonement and satisfaction for all my sins, and for all sins, I offer You Your own holy life, and passion and death. I give to You all the merits and prayers of Mary, Joseph and of all Your dear ones, in time and eternity. In union with all the just in every instant of time, and with all my heart, I believe in You, all truthful; I hope in You, all faithful; I love You, all lovable; and, therefore, I sorrow for all sins. Amen.

In Time of Temptation

Lord and Master, Jesus Christ, who thyself wast tempted as we are, yet without sin, give me grace to meet this temptation which now assails me and which I would overcome. Enable me to check all evil thoughts and passions, all enticements to self-indulgence or dishonest gain, and to find, like thee, my highest satisfactions in the doing of my Heavenly Father's will. Amen.

For Fidelity

Teach us, good Lord, to serve thee as thou deserves; to give and not to count the cost; to fight and not to heed the wounds; to toil and not to seek for rest; to labour and not to ask for any reward, save that of knowing that we do thy will; through Jesus Christ our Lord. Amen.

Prayer For True Manliness

Merciful Jesus, my God and my Lord, Savior of my soul, I ardently beg of You to make me a man, in the truest sense of that noble word, before God and before men, and at every instant of my life and death. Fill me, dear Lord, with Your effective and abounding grace, the fruit of Your sacred Life and Passion, that I may clearly know, and bravely do, all that true manliness requires. Make me great in zeal, intelligent and enlightened in faith, firmly to believe all that You have revealed and Your holy Church teaches. Make me mighty in hope, full of confidence that You will do all that You have promised, will help me in temptation and lift me higher and higher in Your love and service until the end. Above all give me a great and pure love of Your Divine Goodness, for Your own sake, and of all my fellows for the love of You. Fill me with zeal, with love and courage in Your service. Make me an apostle, to help to spread Your holy Truth, a faithful and devoted son of Mother Church in all my days and ways. Help me often to receive You in Holy Communion, to pray to You with manly fervor, to put Your love and service above all earthly things. Keep me Yours, in life and death, that I may glorify You in Heaven, to the utmost of my powers according to Your holy Will forever. All this I beseech through Your own merits and prayers, and the intercession of our Mother Mary and of St. Joseph, and of all Your friends, in time and eternity. For this intention, I believe in You, eternal truth; I hope in You, infinite faithfulness; I love You, adorable lovableness; and, therefore, I sorrow for all sin. Amen.

Prayer For Personal Love of Christ

Jesus, my Savior, lover of my soul, I ardently implore You to give me a great and personal love of You. Most manly and lovable of all our human race, true God and man, send Your abounding and effective grace to help me to form in my mind a just and right conception of Your perfect character and actions. Open before me the truth of Your teaching, the beauty of Your life, the splendor of Your perfections, so that I cannot choose but to love You, with all my heart and always. With sorrow I say with St. Augustine, "Too late and too little have I loved You." But now I firmly purpose and ardently desire to love and imitate You to the utmost of my powers. "Master lead on, and I will follow Thee to the last breath, with love and loyalty." But of myself, sweet Jesus, I am incapable of loving You as I should. Adorable Friend, draw me to Your friendship. Choose me and take me, to be Yours forever. To You I dedicate my body and soul, my life and death, all that I have and am; to be Yours, perfectly and forever. This I desire, for this I pray, through all Your own merits and prayers, and the pleadings of Mary and Joseph and of all Your friends, in time and eternity. For this intention, with all the just forever, I believe in You, all truthfulness; I hope in You, all faithfulness; I love You, all lovableness; and, therefore, I sorrow for all sin. Amen.

The Lay Leader's Handbook 1966

America the Beautiful
Katharine Lee Bates (1910)

O beautiful for spacious skies,
For amber waves of grain,
For purple mountain majesties
Above the fruited plain!

America! America!
God shed His grace on thee,
And crown thy good with brotherhood
From sea to shining sea!

1967

A Good Example

O God, help me to be a good example to others in the barracks, and grant that I may never be ashamed to witness for thee. Help me to know thee better and to please thee in everything I do. Amen.

When Things Go Wrong

O God, when things go wrong and I cannot relax or think clearly, help me to cast myself and my burdens upon thee. Help me to cease struggling and to trust in thy sustaining powers, and give me courage to face myself, my friends, and my work. Amen.

To Serve with Honor

O God, help me to live in such a way that I will always bring honor to thee and to my uniform. Help me to be obedient to the voice of conscience and to serve the highest that I know. Amen.

Encouragement for the Sick

O God, keep me cheerful even when life becomes difficult, and help me to smile even when it is the last thing I feel like doing. Grant that I may be truly grateful for all that the doctors and nurses are doing for me. Amen.

For Upright Living

O God, keep me from looking in the wrong places for the joy of living. Help me to experience the peace of mind and personal satisfaction that comes from a job well done, and grant that I may know the happiness that comes from clean, upright living. Amen.

Chaplain William E. Parsons, Jr.
Meditations for Servicemen, 1967

1974

Thanks Be to God

Thanks be to you, O God, for Jesus Christ, who for the joy that was set before him endured the cross. Thanks be to you for Jesus Christ, who in the cross triumphed over sin and death, principalities and powers, and over all who desire to thwart your will in the world. Thanks be to you, our Father, for Jesus Christ, who in the cross revealed your love for us by dying for the ungodly; yes, even while we were yet sinners, he died for us. Thanks be to you, O God, for you have called us to take up the cross and follow Christ Jesus. Grant that we may, with courage and joy, remain his disciples, for in Christ's name we pray. Amen.

God's Inexpressible Gift

O Lord God, whom no man has seen nor can see, we bless you that you have been pleased to show us yourself in Jesus Christ, your Son. We are grateful that in the fullness of time he came into this world and took upon himself our human nature. In him we see your love for us and are brought into fellowship with you. Accept our thanks, O Father, in thy holy name of Jesus for this your inexpressible gift. Amen.

Book of Worship for United States Forces, 1974

O Beautiful
Katharine L. Bates (1904)

O beautiful for spacious skies,
For amber waves of grain;
For purple mountain majesties
Above the fruited plain!
America! America!
God shed His grace on thee,
And crown thy good with brotherhood,
From sea to shining sea.

1984

Prayer For Our Country

God of our fathers, who gives salvation to nations and strength to governments, bless and safeguard our country, the United States of America, and the people who dwell therein.

May brotherly love ever be found among all the citizens of our land. Implant in the hearts of all the people a steadfast purpose to work as one for the safeguarding of freedom, justice, and peace.

Supreme King of kings, protect and help our President. Shield him against all sickness and injury. Grant to him and to all the constituted office of our government such wisdom and understanding that they may lead our nation in justice and righteousness. In their days and ours may Judah be save and Israel dwell in safety.

In time of war add: We beseech You, O God, to shield and protect our armed forces, in the air, on sea, and on land. Bless them with victory. May it be Your will that the dominion of tyranny and cruelty speedily be brought to an end and the kingdom of righteousness be established on earth with liberty and freedom for all mankind. Amen.

Prayer on Starting a Journey

May it be Your will, Lord my God and God of my ancestors, to lead
me on the way of peace and guide and direct my steps in peace, so
that You will bring me happily to my destination safe and sound.
Save me from danger on the way. Give me good grace, kindness,
and favor, both in Your eyes and in the eyes of all whom I may meet.
Hear this my prayer, for You are a God who listens to the heart's
request. Fulfill for me Your words, "Behold I am sending before
you an angel to guard you on the way and to bring you to the place
which I have prepared." Blessed are You, O Lord, who hearkens to
prayer.

Prayer Book for Jewish Personnel in the
Armed Forces of the United States, 1984

Take My Life and Let it Be
Frances R. Havergal (1874)

Take my life, and let it be consecrated, Lord, to Thee.
Take my moments and my days; let them flow in ceaseless praise.
Take my hands, and let them move at the impulse of Thy love.
Take my feet, and let them be swift and beautiful for Thee.

Take my voice, and let me sing always, only, for my King.
Take my lips, and let them be filled with messages from Thee.
Take my silver and my gold; not a mite would I withhold.
Take my intellect, and use every power as Thou shalt choose.

Take my will, and make it Thine; it shall be no longer mine.
Take my heart, it is Thine own; it shall be Thy royal throne.
Take my love, my Lord, I pour at Thy feet its treasure store.
Take myself, and I will be ever, only, all for Thee.

1988

For the Unity of the Church

Almighty Father, whose blessed Son, before his passion prayer for his disciples that they might be one, as you and he are one: Grant that your Church, being bound together in love and obedience to you, may be united in one body by the one Spirit, that the world may believe in him whom you have sent, your Son Jesus Christ our Lord. Amen.

For the Mission of the Church

O God, you have made of one blood all the peoples of the earth, and sent your blessed Son to preach peace to those who are far off and to those who are near: Grant that people everywhere may seek after you and find you; bring the nations into your fold; pour out your Spirit upon all flesh; and hasten the coming of your kingdom; through Jesus Christ our Lord. Amen

For Our Enemies

O God, the father of all, whose Son commanded us to love our enemies: Lead them and us from prejudice to truth; deliver them and us from hatred, cruelty, and revenge; and in your good time enable us all to stand reconciled before you; through Jesus Christ our Lord. Amen.

For Joy in God's Creation

O Heavenly Father, you have filled the world with beauty: Open our eyes to behold your gracious hand in all your works; that, rejoicing in your whole creation, we may learn to serve you with gladness; for the sake of him through whom all things were made, your Son Jesus Christ our Lord. Amen.

For Peace

Eternal God, in whose perfect kingdom no sword is drawn but the sword of righteousness, no strength known but the strength of love: So mightily spread abroad your Spirit, that all peoples may be gathered under the banner of the Prince of Peace, as children of one Father; to whom be dominion and glory, now and forever. Amen.

For Married Persons

O gracious and ever living God, you have created us male and female in your image: Look mercifully upon (N.) and (N). (or all married persons), and assist them with your grace, that with true fidelity and steadfast love they may honor and keep the promises and vows they have made to each other, through Jesus Christ our Lord. Amen.

For the Care of Children

Almighty God, heavenly Father, you have blessed us with the joy and care of children: Give us calm strength and patient wisdom as we bring them up, that we may teach them to love whatever is just and true and good, following the example of our Savior Jesus Christ. Amen.

For Those We Love

Almighty God, we entrust all who are dear to us to your never-failing care and love, for this life and the life to come, knowing that you are doing for them better things than we can desire or pray for; through Jesus Christ our Lord. Amen.

A Prayer for Mercy and Love

We beseech you, O God, for all prisoners and captives, and for all who suffer from oppression. Show them your mercy and love, we pray and make the hearts of human beings as merciful as your own; through Jesus Christ our Lord. Amen.

For our Country

Lord God Almighty, you have made all the peoples of the earth for your glory, to serve you in freedom and in peace: Give to the people of our country a zeal for justice and strength of forbearance, that we may use our liberty in accordance with your gracious will; through Jesus Christ our Lord. Amen.

A Prayer Book for the Armed Forces, 1988

It Is Well
Horatio Spafford (1873)

When peace like a river, attendeth my way,
When sorrows like sea billows roll;
Whatever my lot, Thou hast taught me to know,
It is well, it is well, with my soul.

   Refrain:
   It is well, with my soul,
   It is well, with my soul,
   It is well, it is well, with my soul.

Though Satan should buffet, though trials should come,
Let this blest assurance control,
That Christ has regarded my helpless estate,
And hath shed His own blood for my soul.

And Lord, haste the day when my faith shall be sight,
The clouds be rolled back as a scroll;
The trump shall resound, and the Lord shall descend,
Even so, it is well with my soul.

2011

Prayer for Those in the Coast Guard

Almighty and Everlasting God, Whose hand stills the tumult of the deep, we offer our prayers for those who serve in our Coast Guard. We are mindful of their traditions of selfless service to the seafarers who make their ways to appointed ports. Employ their devotions of good ends as they track the weather and search for the seas for those in extremity of storm, shipwreck or battle. Make their soundings and markings sure that safe passages may be found by those who go down to the sea in ships. Encourage them, O Lord, as they stand guard over our coasts and the bulwarks of our freedoms. Graciously deliver them from threatening calamities in all their perilous voyages. Bless the keepers of the lights and be Thou their close friend in lonely watches. Keep the beacons of honor and duty burning that they may reach the home port with duty well performed, in service to Thee and our land. AMEN.

From http://www.chaplaincare.navy.mil/index.htm,
Retrieved 2011

Holy, Holy, Holy! Lord God Almighty!
Reginald Heber (1826)

Holy, holy, holy! Lord God Almighty!
Early in the morning our song shall rise to Thee;
Holy, holy, holy, merciful and mighty!
God in three Persons, blessèd Trinity!

Holy, holy, holy! Lord God Almighty!
All Thy works shall praise Thy Name, in earth, and sky, and sea;
Holy, holy, holy; merciful and mighty!
God in three Persons, blessèd Trinity!

PRAYERS BY TOPIC

Prayers By Topic

For Those Who Minister to the Sick and Wounded

In Times of Pain or Affliction

For Times of War

For the United States

For Untroubled Sleep

For Victory

Chaplain of the United States Senate ZeBarney Thorne Phillips
delivering prayer to open the session, 1939.[1]

---

1 From *Traditions of the United States Senate* by Richard A. Baker, Senate Historian.
Prepared under the direction of Nancy Erickson, Secretary of the Senate.

Senior American Commanders and Leaders Who Contributed to Prayer Books

Senior American Commanders and Leaders Who Contributed to Prayer Books

<u>Senior Uniformed Military Authorities</u>
- Brigadier General William R. Arnold
- Omar Bradley, General of the Army, later Chairman of the Joint Chiefs of Staff
- Major General Charles I. Carpenter
- General Clifton B. Cates, Commandant of the Marine Corps
- Mark W. Clark, General of the Army
- General Lucius D. Clay
- General James Lawton Collins, Chief of Staff of the Army
- General Jacob L. Devers, former Chief of Army Field Forces
- Major General John M. Devine
- Dwight D. Eisenhower, General of the Army and Supreme Allied Commander, later President and Commander-in-Chief
- Rear Admiral Thomas L. Gatch
- Vice-Admiral Harry W. Hill, Superintendent, United States Naval Academy
- General Thomas Holcomb, Commandant of the Marine Corps
- Vice-Admiral F. J. Horne, Vice Chief of Naval Operations, United States Navy
- Admiral Ernest J. King, Commander-in-Chief of the United States Fleet and Chief of Naval Operations
- Brigadier General Julius Klein
- Douglas MacArthur, General of the Army
- Captain Thomas MacDonough, before the Battle of Plattsburg, September 11, 1814
- George C. Marshall, General of the Army, Chief of Staff of the Army, later Secretary of State and Defense
- Major General Bryant E. Moore, Superintendent of the United States Military Academy
- Fleet Admiral Chester W. Nimitz
- Vice-Admiral Merlin O'Neill, Commandant of the United States Coast Guard

- Lieutenant General George S. Patton, Jr., Commanding General, United States Army
- Colonel Mary Phillips, Chief of Army Nurse Corps
- Captain Eddie Rickenbacker
- Rear Admiral Stanton W. Salisbury
- Brigadier General La Verne G. Saunders
- Commander Herbert E. Schonland, United States Navy
- Lieutenant Commander Dorothy C. Stratton, Director, Women's Reserve, United States Coast Guard
- United States Navy Prayer for Departing Battalions
- General Hoyt S. Vandenberg, the Commander of the Air Force
- Lieutenant General Alexander A. Vandergrift, Commandant, United States Marine Corps
- Vice Admiral Russell R. Waesche, Commandant of the United States Coast Guard
- General George Washington, Commander-in-Chief

Senior Civilian Military Leaders
- Dean Acheson, the Secretary of State
- Dr. Karl T. Compton, Chairman of the President's Advisory Commission on Universal Military Training
- Thomas K. Finletter, Secretary of the Air Force
- Frank Knox, Secretary of the Navy
- General Curtis E. LeMay, Chief of Staff of the Air Force
- Theus J. MacQueen, National Commander of the Marine Corps League
- Francis P. Matthews, Secretary of the Navy
- Frank Pace, Jr., Secretary of the Army
- Beatrice Patton, widow of General George S. Patton
- Eleanor Roosevelt, wife of Franklin D. Roosevelt
- Harold Russell, National Commander, AMVETS (American Veterans)

Senior Military Chaplains

- Chaplain James L. Blakeney
- Dr. Frederick Brown Harris, Chaplain of the United States Senate
- Major General Luther D. Miller, Chief of Chaplains of the Army
- Dr. James Shera Montgomery, Chaplain of the House of Representatives
- Brigadier General James H. O'Neill, Deputy Chief of Chaplains
- Lieutenant Colonel Samuel Overstreet, Senior Chaplain of the First Division
- Major General Roy H. Parker, Chief of Chaplains
- Reverend Roy B. Schmeichel, the National Chaplain, Veterans of Foreign Wars
- J. Burt Webster, D.D., Chief of Chaplains, Second Service Command, United States Army
- Colonel Clayton E. Wheat, Former Chaplain and Professor of English at West Point
- Captain M.M. Witherspoon, Chaplain, United States Navy

Commanders-in-Chief

- Herbert Hoover, President and Commander-in-Chief
- Franklin Delano Roosevelt, President and Commander-in-Chief

INAUGURAL ADDRESSES

Inaugural Addresses

Excerpts Acknowledging God, His Divine Providence and Prayers
for His Protection from the Inaugural Addresses by Each of Our
Commanders in Chief, from George Washington to Barack Obama

George Washington, First Inaugural Address, April 30th, 1789

"[S]ince we ought to be no less persuaded that the propitious smiles of Heaven can never be expected on a nation that disregards the eternal rules of order and right which Heaven itself has ordained; and since the preservation of the sacred fire of liberty and the destiny of the republican model of government are justly considered, perhaps, as deeply, as finally, staked on the experiment entrusted to the hands of the American people.

Having thus imparted to you my sentiments as they have been awakened by the occasion which brings us together, I shall take my present leave; but not without resorting once more to the benign Parent of the Human Race in humble supplication that, since He has been pleased to favor the American people with opportunities for deliberating in perfect tranquility, and dispositions for deciding with unparalleled unanimity on a form of government for the security of their union and the advancement of their happiness, so His divine blessing may be equally conspicuous in the enlarged views, the temperate consultations, and the wise measures on which the success of this Government must depend."

John Adams, March 4th, 1797

"Relying, however, on the purity of their intentions, the justice of their cause, and the integrity and intelligence of the people, under an overruling Providence which had so signally protected this country from the first, the representatives of this nation, then consisting of little more than half its present number, not only broke to pieces the chains which were forging and the rod of iron that was lifted up, but frankly cut asunder the ties which had bound them, and launched into an ocean of uncertainty.

I feel it to be my duty to add, if a veneration for the religion of a people who profess and call themselves Christians, and a fixed resolution to consider a decent respect for Christianity among the best recommendations for the public service, can enable me in any degree to comply with your wishes, it shall be my strenuous endeavor that this sagacious injunction of the two Houses shall not be without effect.

And may that Being who is supreme over all, the Patron of Order, the Fountain of Justice, and the Protector in all ages of the world of virtuous liberty, continue His blessing upon this nation and its Government and give it all possible success and duration consistent with the ends of His providence."

Thomas Jefferson, First Inaugural Address, March 4th, 1801

"[A]cknowledging and adoring an overruling Providence, which by all its dispensations proves that it delights in the happiness of man here and his greater happiness hereafter--with all these blessings, what more is necessary to make us a happy and a prosperous people?

And may that Infinite Power which rules the destinies of the universe lead our councils to what is best, and give them a favorable issue for your peace and prosperity."

Thomas Jefferson, Second Inaugural Address, March 4th, 1805

"In matters of religion I have considered that its free exercise is placed by the Constitution independent of the powers of the General Government. I have therefore undertaken on no occasion to prescribe the religious exercises suited to it, but have left them, as the Constitution found them, under the direction and discipline of the church or state authorities acknowledged by the several religious societies.

I shall need, too, the favor of that Being in whose hands we are, who led our fathers, as Israel of old, from their native land and planted them in a country flowing with all the necessaries and comforts of life; who has covered our infancy with His providence and our riper years with His wisdom and power, and to whose goodness I ask you to join in supplications with me that He will so enlighten the minds of your servants, guide their councils, and prosper their measures that whatsoever they do shall result in your good, and shall secure to you the peace, friendship, and approbation of all nations."

James Madison, March 4th, 1809

"In these my confidence will under every difficulty be best placed, next to that which we have all been encouraged to feel in the guardianship and guidance of that Almighty Being whose power regulates the destiny of nations, whose blessings have been so conspicuously dispensed to this rising Republic, and to whom we are bound to address our devout gratitude for the past, as well as our fervent supplications and best hopes for the future."

James Monroe, First Inaugural Address, March 4th, 1817

"Relying on the aid to be derived from the other departments of the Government, I enter on the trust to which I have been called by the suffrages of my fellow-citizens with my fervent prayers to the Almighty that He will be graciously pleased to continue to us that protection which He has already so conspicuously displayed in our favor."

James Monroe, Second Inaugural Address, March 5th, 1821

"With full confidence in the continuance of that candor and generous indulgence from my fellow-citizens at large which I have heretofore experienced, and with a firm reliance on the protection of Almighty God, I shall forthwith commence the duties of the high trust to which you have called me."

John Quincy Adams, March 4th, 1825

"The year of jubilee since the first formation of our Union has just elapsed that of the declaration of our independence is at hand. The consummation of both was effected by this Constitution.

To the guidance of the legislative councils, to the assistance of the executive and subordinate departments, to the friendly cooperation of the respective State governments, to the candid and liberal support of the people so far as it may be deserved by honest industry and zeal, I shall look for whatever success may attend my public service; and knowing that "except the Lord keep the city the watchman waketh but in vain," with fervent supplications for His favor, to His overruling providence I commit with humble but fearless confidence my own fate and the future destinies of my country."

Andrew Jackson, First Inaugural Address, March 4th, 1829

"And a firm reliance on the goodness of that Power whose providence mercifully protected our national infancy, and has since upheld our liberties in various vicissitudes, encourages me to offer up my ardent supplications that He will continue to make our beloved country the object of His divine care and gracious benediction."

Andrew Jackson, Second Inaugural Address, March 4th, 1833

"In proportion, therefore, as the General Government encroaches upon the rights of the States, in the same proportion does it impair its own power and detract from its ability to fulfill the purposes of its creation. Solemnly impressed with these considerations, my countrymen will ever find me ready to exercise my constitutional powers in arresting measures which may directly or indirectly encroach upon the rights of the States or tend to consolidate all political power in the General Government.

Finally, it is my most fervent prayer to that Almighty Being before whom I now stand, and who has kept us in His hands from the infancy of our Republic to the present day, that He will so overrule all my intentions and actions and inspire the hearts of my fellow-citizens that we may be preserved from dangers of all kinds and continue forever a united and happy people."

Martin Van Buren, March 4th, 1837

"So sensibly, fellow-citizens, do these circumstances press themselves upon me that I should not dare to enter upon my path of duty did I not look for the generous aid of those who will be associated with me in the various and coordinate branches of the Government; did I not repose with unwavering reliance on the patriotism, the intelligence, and the kindness of a people who never yet deserted a public servant honestly laboring their cause; and, above all, did I not permit myself humbly to hope for the sustaining support of an ever-watchful and beneficent Providence.

For myself, therefore, I desire to declare that the principle that will govern me in the high duty to which my country calls me is a strict adherence to the letter and spirit of the Constitution as it was designed by those who framed it. Looking back to it as a sacred instrument carefully and not easily framed; remembering that it was throughout a work of concession and compromise; viewing it as limited to national objects; regarding it as leaving to the people and the States all power not explicitly parted with, I shall endeavor to preserve, protect, and defend it by anxiously referring to its provision for direction in every action. To matters of domestic concernment which it has entrusted to the Federal Government and to such as relate to our intercourse with foreign nations I shall zealously devote myself; beyond those limits I shall never pass.

Beyond that I only look to the gracious protection of the Divine Being whose strengthening support I humbly solicit, and whom I fervently pray to look down upon us all. May it be among the dispensations of His providence to bless our beloved country with honors and with length of days. May her ways be ways of pleasantness and all her paths be peace!"

William Henry Harrison, March 4th, 1841

"However strong may be my present purpose to realize the expectations of a magnanimous and confiding people, I too well understand the dangerous temptations to which I shall be exposed from the magnitude of the power which it has been the pleasure of the people to commit to my hands not to place my chief confidence upon the aid of that Almighty Power which has hitherto protected me and enabled me to bring to favorable issues other important but still greatly inferior trusts heretofore confided to me by my country.

We admit of no government by divine right, believing that so far as power is concerned the Beneficent Creator has made no distinction amongst men; that all are upon an equality, and that the only legitimate right to govern is an express grant of power from the governed. The Constitution of the United States is the instrument containing this grant of power to the several departments composing the Government.

If parties in a republic are necessary to secure a degree of vigilance sufficient to keep the public functionaries within the bounds of law and duty, at that point their usefulness ends. Beyond that they become destructive of public virtue, the parent of a spirit antagonist to that of liberty, and eventually its inevitable conqueror. We have examples of republics where the love of country and of liberty at one time were the dominant passions of the whole mass of citizens, and yet, with the continuance of the name and forms of free government, not a vestige of these qualities remaining in the bosoms of any one of its citizens. It was the beautiful remark of a distinguished English writer that "in the Roman senate Octavius had a party and Anthony a party, but the Commonwealth had none."

Always the friend of my countrymen, never their flatterer, it becomes my duty to say to them from this high place to which their partiality has exalted me that there exists in the land a spirit hostile to their best interests--hostile to liberty itself. It is a spirit contracted in its views, selfish in its objects. It looks to the aggrandizement of a few even to the destruction of the interests of the whole.

I deem the present occasion sufficiently important and solemn to justify me in expressing to my fellow-citizens a profound reverence for the Christian religion and a thorough conviction that sound morals, religious liberty, and a just sense of religious responsibility are essentially connected with all true and lasting happiness; and to that good Being who has blessed us by the gifts of civil and religious freedom, who watched over and prospered the labors of our fathers and has hitherto preserved to us institutions far exceeding in excellence those of any other people, let us unite in fervently commending every interest of our beloved country in all future time."

James K. Polk, March 4th, 1845

"Confidently relying upon the aid and assistance of the coordinate departments of the Government in conducting our public affairs, I enter upon the discharge of the high duties which have been assigned me by the people, again humbly supplicating that Divine Being who has watched over and protected our beloved country from its infancy to the present hour to continue His gracious benedictions upon us, that we may continue to be a prosperous and happy people."

Zachary Taylor, March 5th, 1849

"In conclusion I congratulate you, my fellow-citizens, upon the high state of prosperity to which the goodness of Divine Providence has conducted our common country."

Franklin Pierce, March 4th, 1853

"The energy with which that great conflict [the Revolutionary War] was opened and, under the guidance of a manifest and beneficent Providence the uncomplaining endurance with which it was prosecuted to its consummation were only surpassed by the wisdom and patriotic spirit of concession which characterized all the counsels of the early fathers.

Let it be impressed upon all hearts that, beautiful as our fabric is, no earthly power or wisdom could ever reunite its broken fragments. Standing, as I do, almost within view of the green slopes of Monticello, and, as it were, within reach of the tomb of Washington, with all the cherished memories of the past gathering around me like so many eloquent voices of exhortation from heaven, I can express no better hope for my country than that the kind Providence which smiled upon our fathers may enable their children to preserve the blessings they have inherited."

James Buchanan, March 4ᵗʰ, 1857

"In entering upon this great office I must humbly invoke the God of our fathers for wisdom and firmness to execute its high and responsible duties in such a manner as to restore harmony and ancient friendship among the people of the several States and to preserve our free institutions throughout many generations."

Abraham Lincoln, First Inaugural Address, March 4ᵗʰ, 1861

"Intelligence, patriotism, Christianity, and a firm reliance on Him who has never yet forsaken this favored land are still competent to adjust in the best way all our present difficulty."

Abraham Lincoln, Second Inaugural Address, March 4ᵗʰ, 1865

"Neither party expected for the war the magnitude or the duration which it has already attained. Neither anticipated that the cause of the conflict might cease with or even before the conflict itself should cease. Each looked for an easier triumph, and a result less fundamental and astounding. Both read the same Bible and pray to the same God, and each invokes His aid against the other. It may seem strange that any men should dare to ask a just God's assistance in wringing their bread from the sweat of other men's faces, but let us judge not, that we be not judged. The prayers of both could not be answered. That of neither has been answered fully.

The Almighty has His own purposes. "Woe unto the world because of offenses; for it must needs be that offenses come, but woe to that man by whom the offense cometh." If we shall suppose that American slavery is one of those offenses which, in the providence of God, must needs come, but which, having continued through His appointed time, He now wills to remove, and that He gives to both North and South this terrible war as the woe due to those by whom the offense came, shall we discern therein any departure from those divine attributes which the believers in a living God always ascribe to Him? Fondly do we hope, fervently do we pray, that this mighty scourge of war may speedily pass away.

Yet, if God wills that it continue until all the wealth piled by the bondsman's two hundred and fifty years of unrequited toil shall be sunk, and until every drop of blood drawn with the lash shall be paid by another drawn with the sword, as was said three thousand years ago, so still it must be said "the judgments of the Lord are true and righteous altogether."

With malice toward none, with charity for all, with firmness in the right as God gives us to see the right, let us strive on to finish the work we are in, to bind up the nation's wounds, to care for him who shall have borne the battle and for his widow and his orphan, to do all which may achieve and cherish a just and lasting peace among ourselves and with all nations."

Ulysses S. Grant, March 4th, 1869

"In conclusion I ask patient forbearance one toward another throughout the land, and a determined effort on the part of every citizen to do his share toward cementing a happy union; and I ask the prayers of the nation to Almighty God in behalf of this consummation."

Ulysses S. Grant, March 4th 1873

Fellow-Citizens:

Under Providence I have been called a second time to act as Executive over this great nation.

Rutherford B. Hayes, March 5, 1877

"Looking for the guidance of that Divine Hand by which the destinies of nations and individuals are shaped, I call upon you, Senators, Representatives, judges, fellow-citizens, here and everywhere, to unite with me in an earnest effort to secure to our country the blessings, not only of material prosperity, but of justice, peace, and union--a union depending not upon the constraint of force, but upon the loving devotion of a free people; "and that all things may be so ordered and settled upon the best and surest foundations that peace and happiness, truth and justice, religion and piety, may be established among us for all generations."

James A. Garfield, March 4, 1881

"Before continuing the onward march let us pause on this height for a moment to strengthen our faith and renew our hope by a glance at the pathway along which our people have traveled.

The emancipated race has already made remarkable progress. With unquestioning devotion to the Union, with a patience and gentleness not born of fear, they have "followed the light as God gave them to see the light."

Let our people find a new meaning in the divine oracle which declares that "a little child shall lead them," for our own little children will soon control the destinies of the Republic.

My countrymen, we do not now differ in our judgment concerning the controversies of past generations, and fifty years hence our children will not be divided in their opinions concerning our controversies. They will surely bless their fathers and their fathers' God that the Union was preserved, that slavery was overthrown, and that both races were made equal before the law.

The Constitution guarantees absolute religious freedom. Congress is prohibited from making any law respecting an establishment of religion or prohibiting the free exercise thereof. The Territories of the United States are subject to the direct legislative authority of Congress, and hence the General Government is responsible for any violation of the Constitution in any of them. It is therefore a reproach to the Government that in the most populous of the Territories the constitutional guaranty is not enjoyed by the people and the authority of Congress is set at naught. The Mormon Church not only offends the moral sense of manhood by sanctioning polygamy, but prevents the administration of justice through ordinary instrumentalities of law.

In my judgment it is the duty of Congress, while respecting to the uttermost the conscientious convictions and religious scruples of every citizen, to prohibit within its jurisdiction all criminal practices, especially of that class which destroy the family relations and endanger social order. Nor can any ecclesiastical organization be safely permitted to usurp in the smallest degree the functions and powers of the National Government.

I shall greatly rely upon the wisdom and patriotism of Congress and of those who may share with me the responsibilities and duties of administration, and, above all, upon our efforts to promote the welfare of this great people and their Government I reverently invoke the support and blessings of Almighty God."

Grover Cleveland, March 4th, 1885

"And let us not trust to human effort alone, but humbly acknowledging the power and goodness of Almighty God, who presides over the destiny of nations, and who has at all times been revealed in our country's history, let us invoke His aid and His blessings upon our labors."

Benjamin Harrison, March 4th, 1889

"Entering thus solemnly into covenant with each other, we may reverently invoke and confidently expect the favor and help of Almighty God--that He will give to me wisdom, strength, and fidelity, and to our people a spirit of fraternity and a love of righteousness and peace.

The influences of religion have been multiplied and strengthened.

God has placed upon our head a diadem and has laid at our feet power and wealth beyond definition or calculation. But we must not forget that we take these gifts upon the condition that justice and mercy shall hold the reins of power and that the upward avenues of hope shall be free to all the people."

Grover Cleveland, Second Inaugural Address, March 4th, 1893

"Deeply moved by the expression of confidence and personal attachment which has called me to this service, I am sure my gratitude can make no better return than the pledge I now give before God and these witnesses of unreserved and complete devotion to the interests and welfare of those who have honored me.

It can not be doubted that our stupendous achievements as a people and our country's robust strength have given rise to heedlessness of those laws governing our national health which we can no more evade than human life can escape the laws of God and nature.

Above all, I know there is a Supreme Being who rules the affairs of men and whose goodness and mercy have always followed the American people, and I know He will not turn from us now if we humbly and reverently seek His powerful aid."

William McKinley, First Inaugural Address, March 4th, 1897

"In obedience to the will of the people, and in their presence, by the authority vested in me by this oath, I assume the arduous and responsible duties of President of the United States, relying upon the support of my countrymen and invoking the guidance of Almighty God. Our faith teaches that there is no safer reliance than upon the God of our fathers, who has so singularly favored the American people in every national trial, and who will not forsake us so long as we obey His commandments and walk humbly in His footsteps.

Let me again repeat the words of the oath administered by the Chief Justice which, in their respective spheres, so far as applicable, I would have all my countrymen observe: "I will faithfully execute the office of President of the United States, and will, to the best of my ability, preserve, protect, and defend the Constitution of the United States." This is the obligation I have reverently taken before the Lord Most High. To keep it will be my single purpose, my constant prayer; and I shall confidently rely upon the forbearance and assistance of all the people in the discharge of my solemn responsibilities."

William McKinley, Second Inaugural Address, March 4th, 1901

"Entrusted by the people for a second time with the office of President, I enter upon its administration appreciating the great responsibilities which attach to this renewed honor and commission, promising unreserved devotion on my part to their faithful discharge and reverently invoking for my guidance the direction and favor of Almighty God.

As heretofore, so hereafter will the nation demonstrate its fitness to administer any new estate which events devolve upon it, and in the fear of God will "take occasion by the hand and make the bounds of freedom wider yet."

Theodore Roosevelt, March 4th, 1905

"My fellow-citizens, no people on earth have more cause to be thankful than ours, and this is said reverently, in no spirit of boastfulness in our own strength, but with gratitude to the Giver of Good who has blessed us with the conditions which have enabled us to achieve so large a measure of well-being and of happiness."

William Howard Taft, March 4th, 1909

"I invoke the considerate sympathy and support of my fellow-citizens and the aid of the Almighty God in the discharge of my responsible duties."

Woodrow Wilson, First Inaugural Address, March 4th, 1913

"I summon all honest men, all patriotic, all forward-looking men, to my side. God helping me, I will not fail them, if they will but counsel and sustain me!"

Woodrow Wilson, Second Inaugural Address, March 5th, 1917

"I pray God I may be given the wisdom and the prudence to do my duty in the true spirit of this great people."

Warren Harding, March 4th, 1921

The oath of office was administered by Chief Justice Edward White, using the Bible from George Washington's first inauguration.

"Standing in this presence, mindful of the solemnity of this occasion, feeling the emotions which no one may know until he senses the great weight of responsibility for himself, I must utter my belief in the divine inspiration of the founding fathers. Surely there must have been God's intent in the making of this new-world Republic.

Ours is an organic law which had but one ambiguity, and we saw that effaced in a baptism of sacrifice and blood, with union maintained, the Nation supreme, and its concord inspiring. We have seen the world rivet its hopeful gaze on the great truths on which the founders wrought. We have seen civil, human, and religious liberty verified and glorified. In the beginning the Old World scoffed at our experiment; today our foundations of political and social belief stand unshaken, a precious inheritance to ourselves, an inspiring example of freedom and civilization to all mankind. Let us express renewed and strengthened devotion, in grateful reverence for the immortal beginning, and utter our confidence in the supreme fulfillment.

The recorded progress of our Republic, materially and spiritually, in itself proves the wisdom of the inherited policy of noninvolvement in Old World affairs.

But America, our America, the America builded on the foundation laid by the inspired fathers, can be a party to no permanent military alliance.

America is ready to encourage, eager to initiate, anxious to participate in any seemly program likely to lessen the probability of war, and promote that brotherhood of mankind which must be God's highest conception of human relationship.

If, despite this attitude, war is again forced upon us, I earnestly hope a way may be found which will unify our individual and collective strength and consecrate all America, materially and spiritually, body and soul, to national defense.

My most reverent prayer for America is for industrial peace, with its rewards, widely and generally distributed, amid the inspirations of equal opportunity.

But with the realization comes the surge of high resolve, and there is reassurance in belief in the God-given destiny of our Republic. If I felt that there is to be sole responsibility in the Executive for the America of tomorrow I should shrink from the burden. But here are a hundred millions, with common concern and shared responsibility, answerable to God and country.

I accept my part with single-mindedness of purpose and humility of spirit, and implore the favor and guidance of God in His Heaven. With these I am unafraid, and confidently face the future.

I have taken the solemn oath of office on that passage of Holy Writ wherein it is asked: "What doth the Lord require of thee but to do justly, and to love mercy, and to walk humbly with thy God?" This I plight to God and country."

Calvin Coolidge, March 4th, 1925

"But if we wish to continue to be distinctively American, we must continue to make that term comprehensive enough to embrace the legitimate desires of a civilized and enlightened people determined in all their relations to pursue a conscientious and religious life.

Here it will continue to stand, seeking peace and prosperity, solicitous for the welfare of the wage earner, promoting enterprise, developing waterways and natural resources, attentive to the intuitive counsel of womanhood, encouraging education, desiring the advancement of religion, supporting the cause of justice and honor among the nations. America seeks no earthly empire built on blood and force. No ambition, no temptation, lures her to thought of foreign dominions. The legions which she sends forth are armed, not with the sword, but with the cross. The higher state to which she seeks the allegiance of all mankind is not of human, but of divine origin. She cherishes no purpose save to merit the favor of Almighty God."

Herbert Hoover, March 4th, 1929

"This occasion is not alone the administration of the most sacred oath which can be assumed by an American citizen. It is a dedication and consecration under God to the highest office in service of our people. I assume this trust in the humility of knowledge that only through the guidance of Almighty Providence can I hope to discharge its ever-increasing burdens.

Ill-considered remedies for our faults bring only penalties after them. But if we hold the faith of the men in our mighty past who created these ideals, we shall leave them heightened and strengthened for our children.

I ask the help of Almighty God in this service to my country to which you have called me."

Franklin D. Roosevelt, First Inaugural Address, March 4th, 1933

"In such a spirit on my part and on yours we face our common difficulties. They concern, thank God, only material things.

Compared with the perils which our forefathers conquered because they believed and were not afraid, we have still much to be thankful for.

In this dedication of a Nation we humbly ask the blessing of God. May He protect each and every one of us. May He guide me in the days to come."

Franklin D. Roosevelt, Second Inaugural Address, January 20th, 1937

"Shall we pause now and turn our back upon the road that lies ahead? Shall we call this the promised land? Or, shall we continue on our way?

While this duty rests upon me I shall do my utmost to speak their purpose and to do their will, seeking Divine guidance to help us each and every one to give light to them that sit in darkness and to guide our feet into the way of peace."

Franklin D. Roosevelt, Third Inaugural Address, January 20th, 1941

"As Americans, we go forward, in the service of our country, by the will of God."

Franklin D. Roosevelt, Fourth Inaugural Address, January 20th, 1945

"As I stand here today, having taken the solemn oath of office in the presence of my fellow countrymen--in the presence of our God--I know that it is America's purpose that we shall not fail.

The Almighty God has blessed our land in many ways. He has given our people stout hearts and strong arms with which to strike mighty blows for freedom and truth. He has given to our country a faith which has become the hope of all peoples in an anguished world.

So we pray to Him now for the vision to see our way clearly--to see the way that leads to a better life for ourselves and for all our fellow men--to the achievement of His will to peace on earth."

Harry S. Truman, January 20ᵗʰ, 1949

The President went to the East Portico of the Capitol to take the oath of office on two Bibles--the personal one he had used for the first oath, and a Gutenberg Bible donated by the citizens of Independence, Missouri.

"In performing the duties of my office, I need the help and prayers of every one of you.

It is fitting, therefore, that we take this occasion to proclaim to the world the essential principles of the faith by which we live, and to declare our aims to all peoples.

The American people stand firm in the faith which has inspired this Nation from the beginning. We believe that all men have a right to equal justice under law and equal opportunity to share in the common good. We believe that all men have the right to freedom of thought and expression. We believe that all men are created equal because they are created in the image of God.

From this faith we will not be moved.

People everywhere are coming to realize that what is involved is material well-being, human dignity, and the right to believe in and worship God.

Our allies are the millions who hunger and thirst after righteousness.

Steadfast in our faith in the Almighty, we will advance toward a world where man's freedom is secure.

To that end we will devote our strength, our resources, and our firmness of resolve. With God's help, the future of mankind will be assured in a world of justice, harmony, and peace."

Dwight D. Eisenhower, First Inaugural Address, January 20th, 1953

The Republican Party successfully promoted the candidacy of the popular General of the Army in the 1952 election over the Democratic candidate, Adlai Stevenson. The oath of office was administered by Chief Justice Frederick Vinson on two Bibles--the one used by George Washington at the first inauguration, and the one General Eisenhower received from his mother upon his graduation from the Military Academy at West Point. A large parade followed the ceremony, and inaugural balls were held at the National Armory and Georgetown University's McDonough Hall.

"My friends, before I begin the expression of those thoughts that I deem appropriate to this moment, would you permit me the privilege of uttering a little private prayer of my own. And I ask that you bow your heads:

Almighty God, as we stand here at this moment my future associates in the executive branch of government join me in beseeching that Thou will make full and complete our dedication to the service of the people in this throng, and their fellow citizens everywhere. Give us, we pray, the power to discern clearly right from wrong, and allow all our words and actions to be governed thereby, and by the laws of this land. Especially we pray that our concern shall be for all the people regardless of station, race, or calling. May cooperation be permitted and be the mutual aim of those who, under the concepts of our Constitution, hold to differing political faiths; so that all may work for the good of our beloved country and Thy glory. Amen. "

Dwight D. Eisenhower, Second Inaugural Address, January 21st, 1957

Chief Justice Earl Warren administered the oath of office on the President's personal Bible from West Point.

Before all else, we seek, upon our common labor as a nation, the blessings of Almighty God. And the hopes in our hearts fashion the deepest prayers of our whole people.

May we pursue the right--without self-righteousness. May we know unity--without conformity. May we grow in strength--without pride in self. May we, in our dealings with all peoples of the earth, ever speak truth and serve justice. And so the prayer of our people carries far beyond our own frontiers, to the wide world of our duty and our destiny.

May the light of freedom, coming to all darkened lands, flame brightly--until at last the darkness is no more.

John F. Kennedy, January 20th, 1961

"For I have sworn I before you and Almighty God the same solemn oath our forebears prescribed nearly a century and three quarters ago.

And yet the same revolutionary beliefs for which our forebears [sic] fought are still at issue around the globe--the belief that the rights of man come not from the generosity of the state, but from the hand of God.

Let both sides unite to heed in all corners of the earth the command of Isaiah--to "undo the heavy burdens ... and to let the oppressed go free."

Now the trumpet summons us again--not as a call to bear arms, though arms we need; not as a call to battle, though embattled we are--but a call to bear the burden of a long twilight struggle, year in and year out, "rejoicing in hope, patient in tribulation"--a struggle against the common enemies of man: tyranny, poverty, disease, and war itself.

With a good conscience our only sure reward, with history the final judge of our deeds, let us go forth to lead the land we love, asking His blessing and His help, but knowing that here on earth God's work must truly be our own."

Lyndon B. Johnson, January 20th, 1965

"On this occasion, the oath I have taken before you and before God is not mine alone, but ours together.

Our destiny in the midst of change will rest on the unchanged character of our people, and on their faith.

But we have no promise from God that our greatness will endure. We have been allowed by Him to seek greatness with the sweat of our hands and the strength of our spirit.

If we fail now, we shall have forgotten in abundance what we learned in hardship: that democracy rests on faith, that freedom asks more than it gives, and that the judgment of God is harshest on those who are most favored.

If we succeed, it will not be because of what we have, but it will be because of what we are; not because of what we own, but, rather because of what we believe.

For we are a nation of believers.

In my lifetime--in depression and in war--they have awaited our defeat. Each time, from the secret places of the American heart, came forth the faith they could not see or that they could not even imagine. It brought us victory. And it will again."

Richard M. Nixon, First Inaugural Address, January 20th, 1969

"Standing in this same place a third of a century ago, Franklin Delano Roosevelt addressed a Nation ravaged by depression and gripped in fear. He could say in surveying the Nation's troubles: "They concern, thank God, only material things."

What remains is to give life to what is in the law: to ensure at last that as all are born equal in dignity before God, all are born equal in dignity before man.

I have taken an oath today in the presence of God and my countrymen to uphold and defend the Constitution of the United States.

Only a few short weeks ago, we shared the glory of man's first sight of the world as God sees it, as a single sphere reflecting light in the darkness. As the Apollo astronauts flew over the moon's gray surface on Christmas Eve, they spoke to us of the beauty of earth-- and in that voice so clear across the lunar distance, we heard them invoke God's blessing on its goodness.

Our destiny offers, not the cup of despair, but the chalice of opportunity. So let us seize it, not in fear, but in gladness-- and, "riders on the earth together," let us go forward, firm in our faith, steadfast in our purpose, cautious of the dangers; but sustained by our confidence in the will of God and the promise of man."

Richard M. Nixon, Second Inaugural Address, January 20th, 1973

"We have the chance today to do more than ever before in our history to make life better in America--to ensure better education, better health, better housing, better transportation, a cleaner environment--to restore respect for law, to make our communities more livable--and to insure the God-given right of every American to full and equal opportunity.

We shall answer to God, to history, and to our conscience for the way in which we use these years.

Today, I ask your prayers that in the years ahead I may have God's help in making decisions that are right for America, and I pray for your help so that together we may be worthy of our challenge.

Let us go forward from here confident in hope, strong in our faith in one another, sustained by our faith in God who created us, and striving always to serve His purpose."

Jimmy Carter, January 20th, 1977

The oath of office was taken on the Bible used in the first inauguration by George Washington

"Here before me is the Bible used in the inauguration of our first President, in 1789, and I have just taken the oath of office on the

Bible my mother gave me a few years ago, opened to a timeless admonition from the ancient prophet Micah: "He hath showed thee, O man, what is good; and what doth the Lord require of thee, but to do justly, and to love mercy, and to walk humbly with thy God."

Ours was the first society openly to define itself in terms of both spirituality and of human liberty.

And I join in the hope that when my time as your President has ended, people might say this about our Nation: that we had remembered the words of Micah and renewed our search for humility, mercy, and justice…"

Ronald Reagan, First Inaugural Address, January 20th, 1981

"Your dreams, your hopes, your goals are going to be the dreams, the hopes, and the goals of this administration, so help me God.

I am told that tens of thousands of prayer meetings are being held on this day, and for that I am deeply grateful. We are a nation under God, and I believe God intended for us to be free. It would be fitting and good, I think, if on each Inauguration Day in future years it should be declared a day of prayer.

The crisis we are facing today…does require, however, our best effort, and our willingness to believe in ourselves and to believe in our capacity to perform great deeds; to believe that together, with God's help, we can and will resolve the problems which now confront us. And, after all, why shouldn't we believe that? We are Americans. God bless you, and thank you."

Ronald Reagan, Second Inaugural Address, January 21st, 1985

January 20th was a Sunday, so Reagan gave his Inaugural Address on the following day.

"God bless you and welcome back. There is, however, one who is not with us today: Representative Gillis Long of Louisiana left us last night. I wonder if we could all join in a moment of silent prayer. (Moment of silent prayer.) Amen.

By 1980, we knew it was time to renew our faith, to strive with all our strength toward the ultimate in individual freedom consistent with an orderly society.

Well, with heart and hand, let us stand as one today: One people under God determined that our future shall be worthy of our past.

My friends, together we can do this, and do it we must, so help me God.

There is no story more heartening in our history than the progress that we have made toward the "brotherhood of man" that God intended for us.

Today, we utter no prayer more fervently than the ancient prayer for peace on Earth.

Now we hear again the echoes of our past: a general falls to his knees in the hard snow of Valley Forge; a lonely President paces the darkened halls, and ponders his struggle to preserve the Union; the men of the Alamo call out encouragement to each other; a settler pushes west and sings a song, and the song echoes out forever and fills the unknowing air.

For all our problems, our differences, we are together as of old, as we raise our voices to the God who is the Author of this most tender music. And may He continue to hold us close as we fill the world with our sound--sound in unity, affection, and love--one people under God, dedicated to the dream of freedom that He has placed in the human heart, called upon now to pass that dream on to a waiting and hopeful world. God bless you and may God bless America."

George Bush, January 20th, 1989

"I have just repeated word for word the oath taken by George Washington 200 years ago, and the Bible on which I placed my hand is the Bible on which he placed his.

And my first act as President is a prayer. I ask you to bow your heads:

Heavenly Father, we bow our heads and thank You for Your love. Accept our thanks for the peace that yields this day and the shared faith that makes its continuance likely. Make us strong to do Your work, willing to heed and hear Your will, and write on our hearts these words: "Use power to help people." For we are given power not to advance our own purposes, nor to make a great show in the world, nor a name. There is but one just use of power, and it is to serve people. Help us to remember it, Lord. Amen.

And if our flaws are endless, God's love is truly boundless.

God bless you and God bless the United States of America.

William J. Clinton, First Inaugural Address, January 20th, 1993

"The Scripture says: "And let us not be weary in well-doing, for in due season we shall reap, if we faint not." From this joyful mountaintop of celebration we hear a call to service in the valley. We have heard the trumpets, we have changed the guard, and now each in our own way, and with God's help, we must answer the call.

Thank you, and God bless you all!"

William J. Clinton, Second Inaugural Address, January 20th, 1997

"Guided by the ancient vision of a promised land, let us set our sights upon a land of new promise.

Our rich texture of racial, religious and political diversity will be a godsend in the 21st century.

May God strengthen our hands for the good work ahead, and always, always bless our America."

George W. Bush, January 20th, 2001

"I know this is in our reach because we are guided by a power larger than ourselves who creates us equal in His image.

And to all nations, we will speak for the values that gave our nation birth.

Abandonment and abuse are not acts of God, they are failures of love.

And some needs and hurts are so deep they will only respond to a mentor's touch or a pastor's prayer. Church and charity, synagogue and mosque lend our communities their humanity, and they will have an honored place in our plans and in our laws.

And I can pledge our nation to a goal: When we see that wounded traveler on the road to Jericho, we will not pass to the other side.

Americans are generous and strong and decent, not because we believe in ourselves, but because we hold beliefs beyond ourselves.

We are not this story's author, who fills time and eternity with his purpose. Yet his purpose is achieved in our duty, and our duty is fulfilled in service to one another.

And an angel still rides in the whirlwind and directs this storm.

God bless you all, and God bless America."

George W. Bush, Second Inaugural Address, January 20th, 2005

On this day, prescribed by law and marked by ceremony, we celebrate the durable wisdom of our Constitution, and recall the deep commitments that unite our country. I am grateful for the honor of this hour, mindful of the consequential times in which we live, and determined to fulfill the oath that I have sworn and you have witnessed.

For a half century, America defended our own freedom by standing watch on distant borders. After the shipwreck of communism came years of relative quiet, years of repose, years of sabbatical - and then there came a day of fire.

America's vital interests and our deepest beliefs are now one. From the day of our Founding, we have proclaimed that every man and woman on this earth has rights, and dignity, and matchless value, because they bear the image of the Maker of Heaven and earth. Across the generations we have proclaimed the imperative of self-government, because no one is fit to be a master, and no one deserves to be a slave. Advancing these ideals is the mission that created our Nation. It is the honorable achievement of our fathers. Now it is the urgent requirement of our nation's security, and the calling of our time.

The rulers of outlaw regimes can know that we still believe as Abraham Lincoln did: "Those who deny freedom to others deserve it not for themselves; and, under the rule of a just God, cannot long retain it."

We go forward with complete confidence in the eventual triumph of freedom. Not because history runs on the wheels of inevitability; it is human choices that move events. Not because we consider ourselves a chosen nation; God moves and chooses as He wills. We have confidence because freedom is the permanent hope of mankind, the hunger in dark places, the longing of the soul. When our Founders declared a new order of the ages; when soldiers died in wave upon wave for a union based on liberty; when citizens marched in peaceful outrage under the banner "Freedom Now" - they were acting on an ancient hope that is meant to be fulfilled. History has an ebb and flow of justice, but history also has a visible direction, set by liberty and the Author of Liberty.

When the Declaration of Independence was first read in public and the Liberty Bell was sounded in celebration, a witness said, "It rang as if it meant something." In our time it means something still. America, in this young century, proclaims liberty throughout all the world, and to all the inhabitants thereof. Renewed in our strength - tested, but not weary - we are ready for the greatest achievements in the history of freedom.

May God bless you, and may He watch over the United States of America.

Barack Obama, January 20, 2009

Forty-four Americans have now taken the presidential oath. The words have been spoken during rising tides of prosperity and the still waters of peace. Yet, every so often the oath is taken amidst gathering clouds and raging storms. At these moments, America has carried on not simply because of the skill or vision of those in high office, but because We the People have remained faithful to the ideals of our forbearers, and true to our founding documents.

We remain a young nation, but in the words of Scripture, the time has come to set aside childish things. The time has come to reaffirm our enduring spirit; to choose our better history; to carry forward that precious gift, that noble idea, passed on from generation to generation: the God-given promise that all are equal, all are free, and all deserve a chance to pursue their full measure of happiness.

Our Founding Fathers, faced with perils we can scarcely imagine, drafted a charter to assure the rule of law and the rights of man, a charter expanded by the blood of generations. Those ideals still light the world, and we will not give them up for expedience's sake.

As we consider the road that unfolds before us, we remember with humble gratitude those brave Americans who, at this very hour, patrol far-off deserts and distant mountains. They have something to tell us today, just as the fallen heroes who lie in Arlington whisper through the ages.

We honor them not only because they are guardians of our liberty, but because they embody the spirit of service; a willingness to find meaning in something greater than themselves. And yet, at this moment - a moment that will define a generation - it is precisely this spirit that must inhabit us all.

For as much as government can do and must do, it is ultimately the faith and determination of the American people upon which this nation relies.

What is required of us now is a new era of responsibility - a recognition, on the part of every American, that we have duties to ourselves, our nation, and the world, duties that we do not grudgingly accept but rather seize gladly, firm in the knowledge that there is nothing so satisfying to the spirit, so defining of our character, than giving our all to a difficult task.

This is the source of our confidence - the knowledge that God calls on us to shape an uncertain destiny.

America...Let it be said by our children's children that when we were tested we refused to let this journey end, that we did not turn back nor did we falter; and with eyes fixed on the horizon and God's grace upon us, we carried forth that great gift of freedom and delivered it safely to future generations.

APPENDIX

President Roosevelt's Commendation

The White House
Washington

March 6, 1941

To the Members of the Army:

As Commander-in-Chief I take pleasure in commending the reading of the Bible to all who serve in the armed forces of the United States. Throughout the centuries men of many faiths and diverse origins have found in the Sacred Book words of wisdom, counsel and inspiration. It is a fountain of strength and now, as always, an aid in attaining the highest aspirations of the human soul.

Very sincerely yours,

Franklin D. Roosevelt

Franklin D. Roosevelt
President of the United States

The New Testament of Our Lord and Saviour Jesus Christ
Prepared for use of Protestant Personnel
of the Army of the United States
Published Under the Direction of the Chief of Chaplains
U.S. GPO, Washington, 1942

The Lord's Prayer

Our Father, which art in heaven, hallowed be
Thy name; Thy kingdom come; Thy will be done,
on earth as it is in heaven. Give us this day our
daily bread. And forgive us our trespasses, as we
forgive those that trespass against us. And lead
us not into temptation; but deliver us from evil.
For Thine is the kingdom, the power, and the
glory, forever and ever. Amen.

The Ten Commandments

On February 2, 1983, President Ronald Regan declared 1983 the "Year of the Bible." The House and Senate passed a joint resolution stating that;

> *...many of our great national leaders – among them Presidents Washington, Jackson, Lincoln, and Wilson – paid tribute to the surpassing influence of the Bible in our country's development, as in the words of President Jackson that the Bible is 'the rock on which our Republic rests....Furthermore, President Reagan has emphasized how fundamental and important the Ten Commandments are to any system of law: 'They say that man has written about four billion laws, and with all the four billion they haven't improved on the Ten Commandments one bit.'*

I. Thou shalt have no other god before Me.

II. Thou shalt not make unto thee any graven image, or any likeness of anything that is in heaven above, or that is in the earth beneath, or that is in the water under the earth: thou shalt not bow down thyself to them, nor serve them: for I the Lord thy God am a jealous God, visiting the inquiry of the fathers upon the children unto the third and fourth generations of them that hate Me; and showing mercy unto thousands of them that love Me, and keep my commandments.

III. Thou shalt not take the Name of the Lord thy God in vain; for the Lord will not hold him guiltless that taketh his Name in vain.

IV. Remember the Sabbath-day, to keep it holy. Six days shalt thou labor, and do all thy work: but the seventh day is the Sabbath of the Lord thy God; in it thou shalt not do any work, thou, nor thy son, nor thy daughter, thy man-servant, nor thy maidservant, nor thy cattle, nor thy stranger that is within thy gates; for in six days the Lord made heaven and earth, the sea, and all that in them is, and rested the seventh day: wherefore the Lord blessed the Sabbath-day, and hallowed it.

V. Honor thy father and mother: that thy days may be long
uponthe land which the Lord thy God giveth thee.

VI. Thou shalt not kill.

VII. Thou shalt not commit adultery.

VIII. Thou shalt not steal.

IX. Thou shalt not bear false witness against thy neighbor.

X. Thou shalt not covet thy neighbor's house, thou shalt not covet
thy neighbor's wife, nor his man-servant, nor his maid-servant,
nor his ox, nor his ass, nor anything that is thy neighbor's.

Song and Service Book for Ship and Field, 1941

"The Year of the Bible" resolution concludes with;

> *The historical importance of the Ten Commandments is even captured
> in the architecture of the U.S. Supreme Court Building. Directly
> above the bench in the Courtroom is a marble sculpture of the Ten
> Commandments tablet between two central figures depicting Majesty of
> the Law and Power of Government.*
>
> *…it would serve an educational purpose for our citizens to become
> familiar with the important role which the Bible and the Ten
> Commandments have played in molding our American traditions and
> laws.'*

The Star Spangled Banner

The lyrics of the United State's National Anthem came from a poem written in 1814 by a 35-year-old lawyer and amateur poet, Francis Scott Key. Following its composition, the poem was printed as a broadside, or a large sheet of paper, used for posters and announcements, entitled:

"Defense of Fort McHenry"

The annexed song was composed under the following circumstances— A gentleman had left Baltimore, in a flag of truce for the purpose of getting released from the British fleet, a friend of his who had been captured at Marlborough. He went as far as the mouth of the Patuxent, and was not permitted to return lest the intended attack on Baltimore should be discolsed. He was therefore brought up the Bay to the mouth of the Patapsco, where the flag vessel was kept under the guns of a frigate, and he was compelled to witness the bombardment of Fort McHenry, which the Admiral had boasted

that he would carry in a few hours, and that the city must fall. He watched the flag at the Fort through the whole day with an anxiety that can be better felt than described, until the night prevented him from seeing it. In the night he watched the Bomb Shells, and at early dawn his eye was again greeted by the proudly waving flag of his country.

Flag that floated over Fort McHenry in 1814

Tune — Aanacreon in Heaven.

Oh, say can you see, by the dawn's early light,
What so proudly we hailed at the twilight's last gleaming?
Whose broad stripes and bright stars, through the perilous fight,
O'er the ramparts we watched, were so gallantly streaming?
And the rockets' red glare, the bombs bursting in air,
Gave proof through the night that our flag was still there.
O say, does that star-spangled banner yet wave
O'er the land of the free and the home of the brave?

On the shore, dimly seen through the mists of the deep,
Where the foe's haughty host in dread silence reposes,
What is that which the breeze, o'er the towering steep,
As it fitfully blows, half conceals, half discloses?
Now it catches the gleam of the morning's first beam,
In full glory reflected now shines on the stream:
'Tis the star-spangled banner! O long may it wave
O'er the land of the free and the home of the brave.

And where is that band who so vauntingly swore
That the havoc of war and the battle's confusion
A home and a country should leave us no more?
Their blood has wiped out their foul footstep's pollution.
No refuge could save the hireling and slave
From the terror of flight, or the gloom of the grave:
And the star-spangled banner in triumph doth wave
O'er the land of the free and the home of the brave.

Oh! thus be it ever, when freemen shall stand
Between their loved homes and the war's desolation!
Blest with victory and peace, may the heaven-rescued land
Praise the Power that hath made and preserved us a nation.
Then conquer we must, when our cause it is just,
And this be our motto: "In God is our trust."
And the star-spangled banner in triumph shall wave
O'er the land of the free and the home of the brave!

How to Use the Bible

- When things go well and the world is good to you, read Deuteronomy 8.
- When you are in trouble and things go against you, read Psalm 27.
- When your faith gets weak, read Hebrews 11.
- When sin troubles you, read Psalm 51; II Samuel 11:12; I John 1:7-10.
- When you are becoming indifferent toward God and religion, read Revelation 3.
- When seeking forgiveness, read Psalm 32; Isaiah 1; I John 1:7-10.
- When you are leaving home, read Psalm 121.
- When you have the blues, read Psalm 34 and John 14.
- If you are discouraged, read Isaiah 40 and Psalm 43.
- When you are lonely and fearful, ready Psalm 23.
- In time of bodily want and economic distress, read Psalm 139; Psalm 42; Psalm 73; Psalm 145, 15:16.
- When in danger, read Psalm 91.
- When you are tempted by sin, read Matthew 4:1-11 and Romans 6.
- When you are sick, ready Matthew 9:1-12; Luke 8:43-48; and Psalm 39 and 91.
- In time of affliction and severe trail, read I Peter 4:12-13; II Corinthians 4:16-18, Romans 8; Isaiah 49:14-16.
- When in sorrow over death, read John 11 and 14; I Corinthians 15; I Thessalonians 4:13-14.
- When you worry, ready Matthew 6:19-34.
- When you grow bitter or critical, read I Corinthians 13.
- When you are weary and heavy laden, read Matthew 11:28-30; and Isaiah 55.
- When you need encouragement to prayer, read Luke 11:1-13 and Matthew 6:5-15.

- If you would know Jesus as your Redeemer and Savior, read Isaiah 53; II Corinthians 5:14, 21; I Peter 3:18; Colossians 1:14; I Peter 1:18-19; Romans 5:8-9.
- When you want strength against worldliness, read I John 2:12-17 and I Timothy 6.

Service Prayer Book, 1940,
Edited by N.M. Ylvisaker – Major Chaplain, O.R.C.

How Does a Christian Enter Into True Christian Prayer on Behalf of His/Her Nation?

First, the Bible states:

· "There is one God, and one mediator between God and men, the man Christ Jesus." (I Timothy 2:5).

When we ask God to intervene on behalf of our Nation, Jesus commanded us to do so in His name—

· "Verily, verily, I say unto you, Whatsoever ye shall ask the Father in my name, he will give it you." (John 16:23).

· It is Jesus Christ himself who appears in the presence of God on our behalf when we pray (Hebrews 9:24).

· We have no hope without Jesus Christ (Ephesians 2:12-13), and when we confess and repent of sin, we find righteousness only through Jesus Christ (Romans 5:17).

· Then the effectual and fervent prayers of a righteous man avail much (James 5:16).

Based on these scriptures, it is abundantly clear that prayers of faith are heard and answered through Jesus Christ, the "Author and Finisher of our faith." Prayer must be offered in Jesus' name, and under His authority, and all other prayers are false, ineffectual and worthless.

BIBLIOGRAPHY & INDEX

Bibliography

Military Prayer Books of the Armed Forces

1643. *A Salve for Every Sore*, A collection of promises out of the whole Book of God and is the Christian centurions infallible ground of conscience, His pore soules most assured comfortable companion at all times and in all things. By Phillip Skippon. London: Printed by E.G. for Samuel Enderby.

*1664. *Souldiers Catechisme*. *The Souldiers Catechisme*, composed for the Parliaments army: consisting of two parts: wherein are chiefly taught, 1. the justification, 2. the qualification of our souldiers: written for the encouragement and instruction of all that have taken up arms in the cause of God and His people. By Robert Ram. London: Reprinted by T.B., and are to be sold by R. Taylor.

1775. Leonard Abiel. (Chaplain to General Putnam's regiment). *A Prayer, Composed for the Benefit of the Soldiery in the American Army, to assist them in their private devotions; and recommended to their particular use.* Cambridge: S. & E. Hall.

*1785. *The Book of Common Prayer: For the Use of the First Episcopal Church in Boston*. This book was published for the oldest Anglican church in Boston, founded in 1686. Boston: Peter Edes, Justus Anglican. Web. <http://justus.anglican.org/resources/bcp/kings_chapel1785.pdf>

1812. *A Sailor's Manual of Prayer for Every Day in the Year.* By William Fox. London: Printed for the author by the Philanthropic Society.

186X. *The Soldier's Text-Book: or, Confidence in Time of War.* J. R. Macduff. Boston: American Tract Society.

1861. *The Soldier's Manual of Devotion.* J. G. Forman. Alton, Illinois: L. A. Parks & Co.

1861. *The Soldier's Friend*. By John W. Dulles. Philadelphia: C.S. Luther.

1861. *Prayers, &c. Suitable for the Times in Which We Live, for the use of the soldiers of the Army of the Confederate States*. Charleston: Evans & Cogswell.

1861. *Prayers and Other Devotions for the Use of the Soldiers of the Army of the Confederate States*. Published for the Female Bible, Prayer-Book and Tract Society. Charleston: Evans & Cogswell.

1861. *The Angel of Prayer: With a Selection of Devotions for Christians*. Richmond: J. W. Randolph. (Original in the Museum of the Confederacy Library, Richmond.)

*1861. *Soldier's Prayer Book: Arranged from the book of Common Prayer with Additional Collects and Hymns*. Philadelphia: Alonzo Potter, Bishop of the Diocese of Penna., Justus Anglican. Web. <http://justus.anglican.org/resources/bcp/1789Selections/Soldiers.html#collects>.

1862. *The Soldier's Hymn-book for Camp Worship*. Richmond: Soldiers' Tract Society, Virginia Conference, Methodist Episcopal Church, South. C. H. Wynne.

1862. *The Soldier's Hymn Book*. Charleston: South Carolina Tract Society, Evans & Cogswell. The 2nd Ed., Revised, was published in 1863, (30,000).

*1862. *Hymns for the Camp*. 2nd Ed., Revised and Enlarged. Raleigh: Strother & Marcom.

1863. *The Soldier's Prayer Book*. Charleston: South Carolina Tract Society, Evans & Cogswell.

1863. *The Soldier's Hymn-book for Camp Worship*. Richmond: Soldier's Tract Association, Virginia Conference, Methodist Episcopal Church, South, Macfarlane & Fergusson.

1863. *The Soldier's Manual of Devotion or Book of Common Prayer*; containing a form of public worship, with responses, additional prayers, a psalter, scripture lessons, articles of religion, and a collection of hymns and national songs. 2nd Ed. St. Louis: A. Wiebusch & Son.

1863. *The Courtland Saunders Tract for Soldiers*. Selections from the Bible made in the camp of the First Corn Exchange Regiment, of Philadelphia (the 118th Regiment, P.V.). Philadelphia: Protestant Episcopal Book Society. Also includes a memorial from one hundred cadets, since styled the Courtland Saunders Cadets.

*1863. *Prayer Book for the Camp*. Diocesan Missionary Society, Protestant Episcopal Church in Virginia. Richmond: Macfarlane & Fergusson.

*1863. *The Confederate Soldier's Prayer Book*: A Manual of Devotions, Compiled Mainly from the Book of Common Prayer and Arranged for Public and Private Use in Camps and Hospitals. Joseph W. Murphy. Petersburg, VA: St. Paul's Congregation.

1863. *The Confederate Soldier's Pocket Manual of Devotions*. C. T. Quintard. Charleston: Evans & Cogswell.

1863. *The Army Hymn-Book*. Richmond, VA: Presbyterian Committee of Publication. (2nd Edition, 1864).

1863. *The Army and Navy Hymn Book*. Petersburg, VA: Evangelical Tract Society.

1864. *The Southern Zion's Songster*: Hymns designed for Sabbath schools, prayer, and social meetings, and the camps. Raleigh: North Carolina Christian Advocate Publishing.

1864. *The Soldier's Hymn-Book for Camp Worship*. Richmond: Soldiers' Tract Association, Methodist Episcopal Church, South.

1864. *Hymns for the Camp*. Raleigh: Biblical Recorder Printing.

*1864. *Balm for the Weary and Wounded.* Rev. C. T. Quintard (Chaplain 1st Tenn. Reg't, C.S.A.) Columbia: Evans & Cogswell.

1864. *The Army and Navy Prayer Book.* Diocesan Missionary Society of the Protestant Episcopal Church of Virginia. Richmond: C. H. Wynne. (Reprinted, 1865).

1900. *Prayers for Public Observances.* Ft. Monmouth, NJ: U.S. Army Chaplain Center and School.

*1917. *For Soldiers and Sailors: An Abridgment of the Book of Common Worship,* published for the National Service Commission of the Presbyterian Church in the United States of America. Philadelphia: Presbyterian Board of Publication.

1917. *Abridged Prayer Book for Jews in the Army and Navy of the United States.* Philadelphia: Jewish Publication Society of America.

1917. *Union Prayer book.* By Cyrus Adler, Bernard Drachman, and William Rosenau. Jewish Publication Society.

A Prayer for Divine Aid (to Be Recited During the War). Louis Ginzberg. New York: The Jewish Theological Seminary. No Date; circa WWI.

*1917. *Army and Navy Service Book.* National Lutheran Commission for Soldiers' and Sailors' Welfare. Printed and distributed by Augsburg Publishing House. Minneapolis.

1917. *A Prayer Book for Soldiers and Sailors.* Philadelphia: Bishop White Prayer Book Society.

1918. *With God in the War.* New York: MacMillan.

1918. *The Campaign Prayer Book.* There is no publication date, but is believed to have been published around 1918. New York City: Thomas Nelson & Sons, Justus Anglican. Web. <http://justus. anglican.org/resources/bcp/1892/Campaign.htm>.

1918. *A Prayer Book for the public and private use of our soldiers and sailors: with Bible readings and hymns.* Philadelphia: Bishop White Prayer Book Society. "This edition is printed for and distributed by the War Commission."

*1925. *The Army and Navy Hymnal.* New York: The Century Co. Compiled by the chaplains of the Army.

*1941. *Song and Service Book for Ship and Field: Army and Navy.* Ivan L. Bennett, (Ed.). New York: A.S. Barnes and Co. Republished in 1942 by the Washington: Government Printing Office.

*1941. *Prayer Book: Abridged for Jews in the Armed Forces of the United States.* NY: National Jewish Welfare Board. (Reprinted in 1943).

1941. *Army Navy Service Book.* Revised Ed. NY: National Lutheran Council. The Castle Press. This book is a revised edition of the 1917 version. Contains scriptures, 62 prayers for public and private use, and hymns for worship.

*1942. *Rations 100 Days: Edited for Servicemen.* New York: Christian Commission for Camp and Defense Communities. Federal Council of Churches of Christ in America.

1942. *Ministering to the Jews in the Armed Forces of the United States.* New York: Jewish Welfare Board.

*1942. *A Prayer Book for Soldiers and Sailors.* Protestant Episcopal Church. New York. Church Pension Fund. (4th ed.). Identified in the forward as a gift from the church to "you who are serving our country in the Army or the Navy."

1942. *On Guard.* Joseph R. Sizoo. New York: Macmillan.

1942. *Service Prayer Book*, dedicated to the Army, Navy, Marine and Air Corps of the United States. N. M. Ylvisaker, Editor. Augsburg Publishing House, Minneapolis. Fourteen printings of this prayer book were published from December, 1940 to October, 1942, totaling 239,500 copies.

1943. *Prayer Book for Catholic Servicemen*. Washington D. C.: National Catholic Community Service.

*1943. *Prayers for Private Devotions in War Time*. Willard L. Sperry. NY: Harper & Brothers. Reprinted in 1991 by The Memorial Church, Harvard University.

1943. *The Armor of God: Reflections and Prayers for Wartime*. Fulton J. sheen. NY: P.J. Kennedy & Sons.

*1943. *Prayer Book for Catholic Servicemen*. Washington D.C.: The National Catholic Community Service.

*1944. *Soldiers' and Sailors' Prayer Book*. Gerald Mygatt. New York: A. A. Knopf.

*1948. *The West Point Prayer Book*. [New York] : Published by Macmillan for the United States *Military* Academy, c1948. viii, 309 p. ; 20 cm.

1944. *Our Sons will Triumph*; from the D-day Prayer of the Commander in chief of the Armed Forces of the United States, Franklin Delano Roosevelt, June sixth, 1944. Arranged by Jack Dixon. New York: Thomas Y. Crowell.

1944. *D-DAY PRAYER by President Franklin D. Roosevelt from the White House - June 6, 1944. Here printed for his friends at Christmastide 1944.* Publisher: Washington: U.S. Government Printing Office.

194X. *A Prayer Book for Soldiers and Sailors*. Tucker, H. St. George (Presenter). Church Pension Fund. 4th edition. Commission of the Protestant Episcopal Church.

*195X. *Armed Forces Hymnal*. United States Department of Defense, Armed Forces Chaplains Board. Washington: Govt. Printing. Doc. No. D 1.2:H 99.

*1951. *The Armed Forces Prayer Book*. 1951. Daniel A. Poling. New York: Prentice-Hall.

*1951 *The Armed Forces Prayer Book*. By The Church Pension Fund for The Armed Forces Division of the Protestant Episcopal Church. New York City: Rev. Henry K. Sherril, 1951. *Justus Anglican*. Web. <http://justus.anglican.org/resources/bcp/1928/AFPB_index.htm

1957. *Armed Services Manual*. Independence, MO: Reorganized Church of Jesus Christ of Latter Day Saints.

1958. *Prayer Book For Jewish Personnel In The Armed Forces Of The United States*, author unknown. Published by the Commission of Jewish Chaplains, 1958.

*1966. *Lay Leader's Handbook*. Washington: U.S. Govt. Printing. Gov. Doc. No. D 214.9/2:L 45.

1967. *A Prayer book for the Armed Forces*. Published for the Bishop for the Armed Forces, the Episcopal Church. NY: Seabury Press.

*1967. *Meditations for Servicemen*. William E. Parsons, Jr. Nashville: Abington Press.

1967. *Catholic Supplement: Armed Forces Hymnal*. United States Dept. of Defense, Armed Forces Chaplains Board. Chicago: F.E.L. Church Publications.

1969. *Strength For Service to God and Country*. By Lawrence P. Fitzgerald. Nashville: Abingdon Press.

1969. *High Holy Day Prayer Book: For the Jewish Personnel in the Armed Forces of the United States*. New York: National Jewish Welfare Board.

1970. *Serviceman's Prayer Book: A Book of Devotions for Those in the Armed Forces*. NY: Word Publishing.

*1974. *Book of Worship for United States Forces: a collection of hymns and worship resources for military personnel of the United States of America*. Washington : U. S. Govt. Print. Office. 815 p. ; 23 cm.

*1984. *Prayer Book for Jewish Personnel in the Armed Forces of the United States*. Stephan O. Parnes, Ed. Prepared by the Commission on Jewish Chaplaincy of the National Jewish Welfare Board.

1985. *For All Who Go Down to the Sea in Ships*. Washington D.C.: Office of the Chief of Naval Operations. Gov. Document # D 207.2:Sh 6/3

1986. *Prayers for the United Ministry Team*. Ft. McPherson, GA: HQ, U.S. Army Forces Command.

*1988. *A Prayer Book for the Armed Forces*. Published for the Bishop of the Armed Forces. The Episcopal Church.

*Books located and used in this prayer book.

Index

I

J

K

L

P

R

S

www.firstprinciplespress.org